Charles Rollin

The Life of Alexander the Great, King of Macedon

Compiled from ancient history

Charles Rollin

The Life of Alexander the Great, King of Macedon
Compiled from ancient history

ISBN/EAN: 9783337245146

Printed in Europe, USA, Canada, Australia, Japan

Cover: Foto ©ninafisch / pixelio.de

More available books at **www.hansebooks.com**

THE LIFE
OF
AL   ER

KIN   ON.

COM   Y.

By

Principal of t   r of Eloqu
Royal College,   adem y of In
and Belles-L

TRANSLATED FROM THE FRENCH.

PROVIDENCE:
Printed by B. WHEEL
For JOSEPH J. TODD
At the BIBLE and ANCHOR.
MDCCXCVI.

CONTENTS.

CT. I. *Alexander's birth. The happy natural inclination of that Prince. Aristotle is appointed his preceptor, who inspires him with a surprising taste for learning. He breaks Bucephalus.* - - - Page 1.

II. *Alexander after the death of Philip ascends the throne at twenty years of age. - He subjects and reduces the nations contiguous to Macedon who had revolted. He goes into Greece to dissolve the alliance formed against him. He possesses himself of, and destroys Thebes, and pardons the Athenians. He gets himself nominated, in the diet or assembly at Corinth, generalissimo of the Greeks against Persia. He returns to Macedon, and makes preparations for carrying his arms into Asia.* - - - 20

III. *Alexander sets out from Macedon upon his expedition against the Persians. He arrives at Ilion, and pays great honour to the tomb of Achilles. He fights the first battle against the Persians at the river Granicus, and obtains a famous victory.* - - - 30

IV. *Alexander conquers the greatest part of Asia-Minor. He falls sick of a mortal distemper, occasioned by bathing in the river Sydnus. Philip the physician cures him in a few days. Alexander passes the streights of Cilicia. Darius advances at the same time. The bold and free*

CONTENTS.

SECT. I. *Alexander's birth. The happy natural inclination of that Prince. Aristotle is appointed his preceptor, who inspires him with a surprising taste for learning. He breaks Bucephalus.* - - - Page 1.

II. *Alexander after the death of Philip ascends the throne at twenty years of age. - He subjects and reduces the nations contiguous to Macedon who had revolted. He goes into Greece to dissolve the alliance formed against him. He possesses himself of, and destroys Thebes, and pardons the Athenians. He gets himself nominated, in the diet or assembly at Corinth, generalissimo of the Greeks against Persia. He returns to Macedon, and makes preparations for carrying his arms into Asia.* - - - 20

III. *Alexander sets out from Macedon upon his expedition against the Persians. He arrives at Ilion, and pays great honour to the tomb of Achilles. He fights the first battle against the Persians at the river Granicus, and obtains a famous victory.* - - - 30

IV. *Alexander conquers the greatest part of Asia-Minor. He falls sick of a mortal distemper, occasioned by bathing in the river Sydnus. Philip the physician cures him in a few days. Alexander passes the streights of Cilicia. Darius advances at the same time. The bold and free*

free answer of Caridemus to that prince, which costs him his life. Description of Darius' march — — — 40

V. *Alexander gains a famous victory over Darius, near the city of Issus. The consequences of that victory.* — — — 58

VI. *Alexander marches victorious into Syria; the treasures deposited in Damascus are delivered to him. Darius writes a letter to Alexander in the most haughty terms, which he answers in the same stile. The gates of the city of Sidon are opened to him. Abdolonymous is placed upon the throne against his will. Alexander lays siege to Tyre, which at last, after having made a vigorous defence, is taken by storm. The fulfilling of the different prophecies relating to Tyre.* — — — 75

VII. *Darius writes a second letter to Alexander. Journey of the latter to Jerusalem. The honour he pays to Jaddus the high priest. He is shewn those prophecies of Daniel which relate to himself. The king grants great privileges to the Jews, but refuses them to the Samaritans. He besieges and takes Gaza, enters Egypt, and subdues that country. He there lays the foundation of Alexandria, then goes into Lybia, where he visits the temple of Jupiter Ammon, and causes himself to be declared the son of that god. His return into Egypt.* 105

VIII. *Alexander, after his return from Egypt, resolves to go in pursuit of Darius, at his setting out he hears of the death of that monarch's queen. He causes the several honours to be paid her which were due to her rank. He*

passes

CONTENTS.

passes the Euphrates and Tygris, and comes up with Darius. The famous battle of Arbela. - - - 120

IX. *Alexander possesses himself of Arbela, Babylon, Susa, Persepolis; and finds immense riches in those cities. In the heat of drinking he sets fire to the Palace of Persepolis.* 137

X. *Darius leaves Ecbatana. He is betrayed and put in chains by Bessus governor of Bactria. The latter, upon Alexander's advancing towards him, flies, after having covered Darius with wounds, who expires a few moments before Alexander's arrival. He sends his corpse to Sysigambis..* - - - 152

XI. *Lacedemonia revolts from the Macedonians, with almost all Peloponnessus. Antipater marches out upon this occasion, defeats the enemy in a battle, in which Agis is killed. Alexander marches against Bessus. Thalestris, queen of the Amazons, comes to visit him from a far country. Alexander, at his return from Parthia, abandons himself to pleasures and excess. He continues his march towards Bessus. Thalestris, queen of the Amazons, comes to visit him from a far country. Alexander, at his return from Parthia, abandons himself to pleasure and excess. He continues his macrh towards Bessus. A pretended conspiracy of Philotas against the king. He and Parmenio his father, are put to death. Alexander subdues several nations. He at last arrives in Bactriana, whither Bessus is brought to him.* 158

XII. *Alexander after taking a great many cities in Bactriana, builds one near the river Iaxarthes, which*

which he calls by his own name. The Scythians alarmed at the building of this city, send ambassadors to the king. He gains a signal victory over the Scythians. He checks and punishes the insurrection of the Sogdians, sends Bessus to Ecbatana, to be put to death, and takes the city of Petra, which was thought impregnable. - - - 176

XIII. *The death of Clitus. Several expeditions of Alexander. He commands worship to be paid to himself, after the manner of the Persians. Discontents arise among the Macedonians. Death of Calisthenes the philosopher.* 190

XIV. *Alexander sets out for India. He besieges and takes several cities which appeared impregnable, and is often in danger of his life. He crosses the river Indus, afterwards the Hydaspes, and gains a signal victory over Porus, whom he restores to his throne.* - - 202

XV. *Alexander advances into India. Resolves to march as far as the Ganges, which raises a general discontent in his army. Remonstrances being made to him on that account, he lays aside his design, and is contented with going no farther than the ocean. He subdues all things in his way thither, and is exposed to great danger at the siege of the city of the Oxydracae; and arriving at last at the ocean, he afterwards prepares for his return into Europe.* 220

XVI. *Alexander, in his march through deserts, is grievously distressed by famine. He arrives at Pasagardae, where Cyrus's monument stood. Orsines, a powerful lord, is put to death by the clandestine intrigues of Bagoas the eunuch. Ca-*

laus the Indian ascends a funeral pile, where he puts himself to death. Alexander marries Statira, the daughter of Darius. Harpalus arrives at Athens; Demosthenes is banished. The Macedonian soldiers make an insurrection, which Alexander appeases. He recalls Antipater from Macedonia, and sends Craterus in his room. The king's sorrow for the death of Hephaestion. - - - - 232

II. Alexander enters Babylon, contrary to the sinister predictions of the Magi and Soothsayers. He there forms the plan of several voyages and conquests. He sets about repairing the breaches made in the piers of the Tygris and Euphrates, and rebuilding the temple of Balus. He abandons himself to immoderate drinking, which brings him to his end. The universal grief spread over the whole empire upon that account. Sysigambis is not able to survive him. Preparations are made to convey Alexander's corps to the temple of Jupiter-Ammon, in Libya. 247

THE LIFE OF ALEXANDER.

BOOK I.

SECT. I. *Alexander's birth. The happy natural inclination of that Prince. Aristotle is appointed his preceptor, who inspires him with a surprising taste for learning. He breaks Bucephalus.*

ALEXANDER came into the world the first year of the CVIth Olympiad.

The passion which ever prevailed most in Alexander, even from his tender years, was ambition, and an ardent desire of glory; but not for every species of glory. Philip (his father) like a sophist, valued himself upon his eloquence and the beauty of his stile; and had the vanity to have engraved on his coins the several victories he had won at the Olympick games in the Chariot-race. But it was not to this his son aspired. His friends asking him one day whether he would not be present at the games above-mentioned, in order to dispute the

THE LIFE OF ALEXANDER.

BOOK I.

SECT. I. *Alexander's birth. The happy natural inclination of that Prince. Ariftotle is appointed his preceptor, who infpires him with a furprifing tafte for learning. He breaks Bucephalus.*

ALEXANDER came into the world the firſt year of the CVIth Olympiad.

The paſſion which ever prevailed moſt in Alexander, even from his tender years, was ambition, and an ardent deſire of glory; but not for every ſpecies of glory. Philip (his father) like a ſophiſt, valued himſelf upon his eloquence and the beauty of his ſtile; and had the vanity to have engraved on his coins the ſeveral victories he had won at the Olympick games in the Chariot-race. But it was not to this his ſon aſpired. His friends aſking him one day whether he would not be preſent at the games above-mentioned, in order to diſpute the prize

prize bestowed on that occasion? for he was very swift of foot, He answered, That he would contend in them, provided kings were to be his antagonists.

Every time news was brought him that his father had taken some city, or gained some great battle, Alexander so far from sharing in the general joy, used to say in a plaintive tone of voice, to the young persons who were brought up with him, friends, my father will possess himself of every thing, and leave nothing for us to do.

One day some ambassadors from the king of Persia being arrived at court during Philip's absence, Alexander gave them so kind and so polite a reception, and regaled them in so noble and generous a manner, as charmed them all; but that which most surprised them was, the good sense and judgment he discovered in the several conversations they had with him. He did not propose to them any thing that was trifling, and like one of his age; but enquired the roads to Upper Asia; the distance of the several places; in what the strength and power of the king of Persia consisted; in what part of the battle he fought; how he behaved towards his enemies; and in what manner he governed his subjects. These ambassadors admired him all the while; and perceiving even at that time how great he might one day become, they observed in a few words, the difference they found between Alexander and Artaxerxes, by saying one to another, This young prince is great, and our's is rich. That man must be vastly insignificant, who has no other merit than his riches!

So ripe a judgment in this young prince, was owing as much to the good education which had been given him, as to the happiness of his natural parts.

Several

Several preceptors were appointed to teach him all such arts and sciences as are worthy the heir of a great kingdom; and the chief of these was Leonidas, a person of the most severe morals and a relation of the queen. Alexander himself tells us afterwards, that this Leonidas, in their journies together, used frequently to look into the trunks where his beds and clothes were laid, in order to see if Olympias his mother had not put something superfluous into them, which might administer to delicacy and luxury.

But the greatest service Philip did his son, was appointing Aristotle his preceptor, the most famous and the most learned philosopher of his age, whom he entrusted with the whole care of his education. One of the reasons which prompted Philip to choose him a master of so conspicuous a reputation and merit was, as he himself tells us, that his son might avoid committing a great many faults of which he himself had been guilty.

Philip was sensible how great a treasure he possessed in the person of Aristotle; for which reason he settled a very considerable stipend upon him, and afterwards rewarded his pains and care in an infinitely more glorious manner; for having destroyed and laid waste the city of Stagira, the native place of that philosopher, he rebuilt it, purely out of affection for him; reinstated the inhabitants who had fled from it, or were made slaves; and gave them a fine park in the neighbourhood of Stagira, as a place for their studies and assemblies. Even in Plutarch's time, the stone seats which Aristotle had placed there were standing; as also spacious vistoes, under which those who walked were shaded from the sunbeams.

Alexander

Alexander likewise discovered no less esteem for his master, whom he believed himself bound to love as much as if he had been his father; declaring that he was indebted to the one for living; and to the other for living well. The progress of the pupil was equal to the care and abilities of the preceptor. He grew vastly fond of philosophy; and learned the several parts of it, but in a manner suitable to his birth. Aristotle endeavoured to improve his judgment, by laying down sure and certain rules, by which he might distinguish just and solid reasoning from what is but speciously so; and, by accustoming him to separate in discourse all such parts as only dazzle from those which are truly solid, and should constitute its whole value.

The greatest master of rhetoric that antiquity could ever boast, took care to make that science part of his pupil's education; and we find that Alexander, even in the midst of his conquests, was often very urgent with Aristotle, to send him a treatise on that subject. To this we owe the work entitled Alexander's Rhetoric, in the beginning of which, Aristotle proves to him the vast advantages a friend may reap from eloquence, as it gives him the greatest ascendant over the minds of men, which he ought to acquire as well by his wisdom as by authority. Some answers and letters of Alexander, which are still extant, show that he possessed, in the greatest perfection, that strong, that manly eloquence, which abounds with sense and ideas; and which is so entirely free from superfluous expressions, that every single word has its meaning; which, properly speaking, is the eloquence of kings.

He

He had also a taste for the whole circle of arts, but in such a manner as became a prince; that is, he knew the value and usefulness of them. Music, painting, sculpture, architecture, flourished in his reign, because they found in him both a skilful judge, and a generous protector, who was able to distinguish and reward merit.

But he despised certain trifling feats of dexterity, that were of no use. Some Macedonians admired very much a man, who employed himself very attentively in throwing small peas through the eye of a needle, which he would do at a considerable distance, and without once missing. Alexander seeing him at this exercise, ordered him, as we are told, a present, suitable to his employment, viz. a basket of peas.

Alexander was of a sprightly disposition; was resolute, and very tenacious of his opinion, which never gave way to force, but at the same time would submit immediately to reason and good sense. It is very difficult to treat with persons of this turn of mind. Philip accordingly, notwithstanding his double authority of king and father, believed it necessary to employ persuasion rather than force, with respect to his son, and endeavoured to make himself beloved rather than feared by him.

An accident made him entertain a very advantageous opinion of Alexander. There had been sent from Thessaly to Philip a war-horse, a noble, strong, fiery, generous beast, called Bucephalus. The owner would sell him for thirteen talents, about 1900l. sterling. The king went into the plains, attended by his courtiers, in order to view the perfections of this horse; but upon trial he appeared so very fierce, and pranced about in so very furious a manner, that no one dared to mount him. Philip, being angry that so furious and unmanageable a creature had been sent him, gave orders for their carrying him back again. Alexander, who was present at that time, cried out, What a noble horse they are going to lose, for want of addrefs and boldness to back him! Philip, at first, considered these words as the effect of folly and rashness, so common to young men: but as Alexander insisted still more upon what he had said, and was very much vexed to see so noble a creature just going to be sent home again, his father gave him leave to try what he could do. The young prince overjoyed at this permission, goes up to Bucephalus, takes hold of his bridle, and turns his head to the sun; having observed the thing which frighted him was his own shadow, he seeing it dance about, or sink down, in proportion as he moved. He, therefore, first stroked him gently with his hand, and soothed him with his voice, then seeing his metal abate, and artfully taking his opportunity, he let fall his cloak, and springing upon his back, first slackened the rein, without once striking or vexing him: and when he perceived that his fire was cooled, that he was no longer so furious and violent, and wanted only to move forward, he gave him the rein, and spurring him with great vigour, animated him with his voice to his full speed. While this was doing, Philip and his whole court trembled with fear, and did not once open their lips; but when the prince, after having run his first heat, returned with joy and pride, at his having broke a horse which was judged absolutely ungovernable, all

the

the courtiers in general endeavoured to outvie one another in their applauses and congratulations; and we are told Philip shed tears of joy on the occasion, and embracing Alexander after he was alighted, and kissing his head, he said to him, My son, seek a kingdom more worthy of thee, for Macedon is below thy merit.

We are told a great many surprising particulars of this Bucephalus; that when this creature was saddled and equipped for battle, he would suffer no one to back him but his master; and it would not have been safe for any person to go near him. Whenever Alexander wanted to mount him, he would kneel down upon his two fore-feet. According to some historians, in the battle against Porus, where Alexander had plunged too imprudently amidst a body of the enemy, his horse, though wounded in every part of his body, did however exert himself in so vigorous a manner, that he saved his master's life; and notwithstanding the deep wounds he had received, and though almost spent through the great effusion of blood, he brought off Alexander from among the combatants, and carried him with inexpressible vigour to a place of security; where perceiving the king was no longer in danger, and overjoyed in some measure at the service he had done him, he expired. Others say, that Bucephalus, quite worn out, died at thirty years of age. Alexander bewailed his death bitterly, believing that he had lost in him a most faithful and affectionate friend; and afterwards built a city on the very spot where he was buried, near the river Hydraspes, and called it Bucephalia, in honour of him.

Alexander,

Alexander, at sixteen years of age, was appointed regent of Macedonia, and invested with absolute authority during his father's absence; he behaved with great prudence and bravery; and afterwards distinguished himself in a most signal manner at the battle of Chæronea.

◦≫◦≪◦

SECT. II. *Alexander after the death of Philip ascends the throne at twenty years of age. He subjects and reduces the nations contiguous to Macedon who had revolted. He goes into Greece to dissolve the alliance formed against him. He possesses himself of, and destroys Thebes, and pardons the Athenians. He gets himself nominated, in the diet or assembly at Corinth, generalissimo of the Greeks against Persia. He returns to Macedon, and makes preparations for carrying his arms into Asia.*

(a) DARIUS and Alexander began to reign the same year: the latter was but twenty, when he succeeded to the crown. His first care was to solemnize the funeral obsequies of his father with the utmost pomp, and revenge his death.

Upon his accession to the throne, he saw himself surrounded with extreme danger. The barbarous nations against whom Philip had fought during his whole reign, and from whom he had made several conquests, which he had united to his crown, after having dethroned their natural kings, thought proper to take the advantage of this juncture, in which a new prince who was but young, had ascended the throne, for recovering their liberty, and uniting

against

(a) *A. M.* 3668. *Ant. J. C.* 386.

against the common usurper. Nor was he under less apprehensions from Greece. Philip, though he had permitted the several cities and commonwealths to continue their ancient form of government, had however, changed it in reality, and made himself absolute master of it. Though he were absent, he nevertheless ruled in all the assemblies; and not a single resolution was taken, but in subordination to his will. Though he had subdued all Greece, either by the terror of his arms, or the secret machinations of his policy, he had not had time sufficient to subject and accustom it to his power, but had left all things in it in great foment and disorder, the minds of the vanquished not being yet calmed nor moulded to subjection.

The Macedonians reflecting on this precarious situation of things, advised Alexander to relinquish Greece, and not persist in his resolution of subduing it by force; to recover by gentle methods the Barbarians who had taken arms, and to soothe, as it were, those glimmerings of revolt and innovation by prudent reserve, complacency, and insinuations, in order to conciliate affection. However, Alexander would not listen to these timorous counsels, but resolved to secure and support his affairs by boldness and magnanimity; firmly persuaded, that should he relax in any point at first, all his neighbours would fall upon him; and that were he to endeavour to compromise matters, he should be obliged to give up all Philip's conquests, and by that means confine his dominions to the narrow limits of Macedon. He, therefore, made all possible haste to check the arms of the Barbarians, by marching his troops to the banks of the Danube, which he crossed in one night. He defeated the king of the Triballi in a great battle; made the Getæ fly at his approach; subdued several barbarous nations, some by the terror of his name, and others by the force of his arms; and notwithstanding the arrogant * answer of the ambassadors, he taught them to dread a danger still more near them than the falling of the sky and planets.

While Alexander was thus employed at a distance against the Barbarians, all the cities of Greece, who were animated more particularly by Demosthenes, formed a powerful alliance against that prince. A false report, which prevailed of his death, inspired the Thebans with a boldness which proved their ruin. They cut to pieces part of the Macedonian garrison in their citadel. Demosthenes, on the other side was every day harranguing the people; and fired with contempt for Alexander, whom he called a child and a hair-brained boy, he assured the Athenians, with a decisive tone of voice, that they had nothing to fear from the new king of Macedon, who did not dare to stir out of his kingdom; but would think himself vastly happy, could he sit peaceably on his throne. At the same time he writ letters upon letters to Attalus, one of Philip's lieutenants in Asia-Minor, to excite him to rebel. This Attalus was uncle to Cleopatra, Philip's second wife, and was very much disposed to listen to Demosthenes' proposal. Nevertheless, as Alexander was grown very diffident of him, for which he knew there was but too much reason; he, therefore, to eradicate from his mind all the suspicions

---

* *Alexander imagining that his name only had struck those people with terror, asked their ambassadors what things they dreaded most: they replied with a haughty tone of voice, that they were afraid of nothing but the falling of the sky and stars.*

picions he might entertain, and the better to screen his design, sent all Demosthenes' letters to that prince. But Alexander saw through all his artifices, and thereupon ordered Hecatæus, one of his commanders, whom he had sent into Asia for that purpose, to have him assassinated, which was executed accordingly. Attalus's death restored tranquility to the army, and entirely destroyed the seeds of discord and rebellion.

(*b*) When Alexander had secured his kingdom from the Barbarians, he marched with the utmost expedition towards Greece, and passed the Thermopylæ. He then spoke as follows to those who accompanied him : Demosthenes called me, in his orations a child, when I was in Illyria, and among the Triballi.; he called me a young man when I was in Thessaly ; and I must now show him, before the walls of Athens that I am a man grown. He appeared so suddenly in Bœtia, that the Thebans could scarce believe their eyes ; and being come before their walls, was willing to give them time to repent, and only demanded to have Phœnix and Prothutes, the two chief ringleaders of the revolt, delivered up to him, and published, by sound of trumpet, a general pardon to all who should come over to him. But the Thebans, by way of insult, demanded to have Philotas and Antipater delivered to them ; and invited, by a declaration, all who were solicitous for the liberty of Greece, to join with them in its defence.

Alexander, finding it impossible for him to get the better of their obstinacy by offers of peace, and saw with grief, that he should be forced to employ his power, and decide the affair by force of arms.

(*b*) A. M. 3670. Ant. J. C. 334.

A great battle was thereupon fought, in which the Thebans exerted themselves with a bravery and ardour much beyond their strength, for the enemy exceeded them vastly in numbers: but after a long and vigorous resistance, such as survived of the Macedonian garrison in the citadel, coming down from it, and charging the Thebans in the rear, surrounded on all sides, the greatest part of them were cut to pieces, and the city was taken and plundered.

It would be impossible for words to express the dreadful calamities which the Thebans suffered on this occasion. Some Thracians having pulled down the house of a virtuous lady of quality, Timoclea by name, carried off all her goods and treasures; and their captain having seized the lady, and satiated his brutal lust with her, afterwards enquired whether she had not concealed gold and silver. Timoclea, animated by an ardent desire of revenge, replying that she had hid some, took him with herself only into her garden, and showing him a well, told him, that the instant she saw the enemy enter the city, she herself had thrown into it the most valuable things in her possession. The officer overjoyed at what he had heard, drew near the well, and stooping down to see its depth, Timoclea who was behind, pushing him with all her strength, threw him into the well, and afterwards killed him with great stones which she threw upon him. She was instantly seized by the Thracians, and being bound in chains, was carried before Alexander. The prince perceived immediately by her mien, that she was a woman of quality and great spirit, for she followed those brutal wretches with a very haughty air, and without discovering the least fear. Alexander asking who she was, Timoclea
replied,

replied, I am sister to Theagenes, who fought against Philip for the liberty of Greece, and was killed in the battle of Chœronea, where he commanded. The prince, admiring the generous answer of that lady, and still more the action she had done, gave orders that she should have leave to retire wherever she pleased with her children.

Alexander then debated in council, how to act with regard to Thebes. The Phocœans and the people of Platæ, Thespiæ, and Orchemenus, who were all in alliance with Alexander, and had shared in his victory, represented to him the cruel treatment they had met with from the Thebans, who also had destroyed their several cities; and reproached them with a zeal which they had always discovered, in favour of the Persians against the Greeks, who held them in the utmost detestation; the proof of which was, the oath they all had taken to destroy Thebes, after they should have vanquished the Persians.

Cleades, one of the prisoners, being permitted to speak, endeavoured to excuse in some measure, the revolt of the Thebans; a fault, which, in his opinion, should be imputed to a rash and credulous imprudence, rather than to depravity of will and declared perfidy. He remonstrated, that his countrymen, upon a false report of Alexander's death, had indeed too rashly broke into a rebellion, not against the king, but against his successors. That what crimes soever they had committed, they had been punished for them with the utmost severity, by the dreadful calamity which had befallen their city. That there now remained in it none but women, children, and old men, from whom they had nothing to fear; and were so much the greater objects of compassion, as they had been no ways concerned in the revolt. He concluded with reminding Alexander, that Thebes, which had given birth to so many Gods and heroes, several of whom were that king's ancestors, had also been the seat of his father Philip's rising glory, and like a second native country to him.

These motives, which Cleades urged, were very strong and powerful; nevertheless, the anger of a conqueror prevailed, and the city was destroyed. However he set at liberty the priests; all such as had right to hospitality, with the Macedonians; the descendants of Pindar, the famous poet, who had done so much honour to Greece; and such as had opposed the revolt: but all the rest, in number about thirty thousand, he sold, and upwards of six thousand had been killed in battle. The Athenians were so sensibly afflicted at the sad disaster which had befallen Thebes, that being about to solemnize the festival of the great mysteries, they suspended them, upon account of their extreme grief, and received with the greatest humanity all those who had fled from the battle, and the plunder of Thebes, and made Athens their asylum.

Alexander's so sudden arrival in Greece, had very much abated the haughtiness of the Athenians, and extinguished Demosthenes' vehemence and fire; but the ruin of Thebes, which was still more sudden, threw them into the utmost consternation. They, therefore, had recourse to entreaties, and sent a deputation to Alexander, to implore his clemency. Demosthenes was among them; but he was no sooner arrived at Mount-Cytheron, than dreading the anger of that prince, he quitted the embassy and returned home. Immediately

Immediately Alexander sent to Athens, requiring the citizens to deliver up to him ten orators, whom he suppofed to have been chief inftruments in forming the league which Philip his father had defeated at Chœrona. It was on this occafion Demofthenes related to the people the fable of the wolves and dogs, in which it is fuppofed, That the wolves one day told the fheep, that in cafe they defired to be at peace with them, they muft deliver up to them the dogs who were their guard. The application was eafy and natural, efpecially with refpect to the orators, who were juftly compared to dogs, whofe duty is to watch, to bark, and to fight, in order to fave the lives of the flock.

In this prodigious dilemma of the Athenians, who could not prevail with themfelves to deliver up their orators to certain death, though they had no other way to fave their city, Demades, whom Alexander had honoured with his friendfhip, offered to undertake the embaffy alone, and to intercede for them, the king, whether he had fatiated his revenge, or endeavoured to blot out if poffible, by fome act of clemency, the barbarous action he had juft before committed; or rather, to remove the feveral obftacles which might retard the execution of his grand defign, and by that means not leave, during his abfence, the leaft pretence for murmurs, waved his demand with regard to the delivery of the orators, and was pacified by their fending Caridemus into banifhment, who being a native of Orea, had been prefented by the Athenians with his freedom, for the fervices he had done the republick. He was fon in law to Cherfobleptus, king of Thrace; had learned the art of war under Iphicrates, and had himfelf frequently

quently commanded the Athenian armies. To avoid the pursuit of Alexander, he took refuge with the king of Persia.

As for the Athenians, he not only forgave the several injuries he pretended to have received, but expressed a particular regard for them, exhorting them to apply themselves vigorously to public affairs, and to keep a watchful eye over the several transactions which might happen; because, in case of his death, their city was to give laws to the rest of Greece. Historians relate, that many years after this expedition, he was seized with deep remorse for the calamity he had brought upon the Thebans, and that this made him behave with much greater humanity towards many other nations.

So dreadful an example of severity towards so powerful a city as Thebes, spread the terror of his arms through all Greece, and made all things give way before him; he summoned at Corinth, the assembly of the several states and free cities of Greece, to obtain from them the same supreme command against the Persians as had been granted his father a little before his death. No diet ever debated on a more important subject. It was the western world deliberating upon the ruin of the east, and the methods for executing a revenge suspended more than an age. The assembly held at this time, will give rise to events, the relation of which will appear astonishing and almost incredible; and to revolutions, which will change the disposition of most things in the world.

To form such a design required a prince bold, enterprising and experienced in war; such a prince was Alexander. It was not difficult for him to rekindle in the minds of the people their ancient hatred of the Persians, their perpetual and irreconcileable enemies; whose destruction they had more than once swore. The deliberations of the assembly were therefore very short, and that prince was unanimously appointed generalissimo against the Persians.

Immediately a great number of officers and governors of cities, with many philosophers, waited upon Alexander to congratulate him upon his election. He flattered himself, that Diogenes of Synope, who was then at Corinth, would also come like the rest and pay his compliments. This philosopher, who entertained a very mean idea of grandeur, thought it improper to congratulate men just upon their exaltation; but that mankind ought to wait till those persons have performed actions worthy of their high stations. Diogenes therefore did not stir out of his house; upon which Alexander, attended by all his courtiers, made him a visit. The philosopher was at that time lying down in the sun; but seeing so great a crowd of people advancing towards him, he set up and fixed his eyes on Alexander. This prince surprised to see so famous a philosopher reduced to such extreme poverty, after saluting him in the kindest manner, asked whether he wanted any thing? Diogenes replied, Yes, that you would stand a little out of my sunshine. This answer raised the contempt and indignation of all the courtiers; but the monarch, struck with the philosopher's greatness of soul, Were I not Alexander, says he, I would be Diogenes. A very profound sense lies hid in this expression, which shews perfectly the bent and disposition of the heart of man. Alexander is sensible that he is formed to possess all things; such is his destiny,

destiny, in which he makes his happiness consist; but then in case he should not be able to compass his ends, he is also sensible, that to be happy, he must endeavour to bring his mind to such a frame as to want nothing. In a word, all or nothing presents us with the true image of Alexander and Diogenes. How great and powerful soever that prince might think himself, he could not deny himself, on this occasion, inferior to a man, to whom he could give, and from whom he could take, nothing.

Alexander, before he set out for Asia, was determined to consult the oracle of Apollo. He therefore went to Delphos; he happened to arrive at it on those days which are called unlucky, a season in which people forbid consulting the oracle; and accordingly the priestess refused to go to the temple. But Alexander, who could not bear any contradiction to his will, took her forcibly by the arm; and, as he was leading her to the temple, she cried out, My son, thou art irresistible. This was all he desired; and catching hold of these words, which he considered as spoke by the oracle, he set out for Macedonia, in order to make preparations for his great expedition.

Sec. III. *Alexander sets out from Macedon upon his expedition against the Persians. He arrives at Ilion, and pays great honour to the tomb of Achilles. He fights the first battle against the Persians at the river Granicnus, and obtains a famous victory.*

(c) ALEXANDER, being arrived in this kingdom, held a council with the chief officers of his army, and
the

(c) *A. M.* 3670. *Ant. J. C.* 334.

the grandees of his court, on the expedition he meditated against Persia, and the measures he should take in order to succeed in it. The whole assembly was unanimous, except on one article. Antipater and Parmenio were of opinion, that the king, before he engaged in an enterprize which would necessarily be a long one, ought to make choice of a consort in order to secure himself a successor to his throne. But Alexander, who was of a violent fiery temper, did not approve of this advice; and believed, that after he had been denominated generalissimo of the Greeks, and that his father had left him an invincible army, it would be a shame for him to lose time in solemnising his nuptials, and waiting for the fruits of it; for which reason he determined to set out immediately.

Accordingly he offered up very splendid sacrifices to the gods, and caused to be celebrated at Dia, a city of Macedon,* scenical games, that had been instituted by one of his ancestors in honor of Jupiter and the muses. This festival continued nine days, agreeable to the number of these goddesses. He had a tent raised large enough to hold a hundred tables, on which consequently nine hundred covers might be laid. To this feast, the several princes of his family, all the ambassadors, generals, and officers, were invited. He also treated his whole army. It was then he had the famous vision, in which he was exhorted to march speedily into Asia, of which mention will be made in the sequel.

Before he set out upon this expedition, he settled the affairs of Macedon, over which he appointed Antipater as viceroy, with twelve thousand foot, and near the same number of horse.

He

---

* *Theatrical representations were so called.*

He also enquired into the domestic affairs of his friends, giving to one an estate in land, to another a village, to a third the revenues of a town, to a fourth, the toll of an harbour, and as all the revenues of his demesnes were already employed and exhausted by his donations, Perdicas said to him, My lord what is it you reserve for yourself! Alexander replying, hope; says Perdicas, the same hope ought therefore to satisfy us: and so refused very generously to accept of what the king had appointed him.

Alexander, after having settled affairs in Macedonia, and used all the precautions imaginable, to prevent any troubles from arising in it during his absence, set out for Asia in the beginning of the spring. His army consisted of little more than thirty thousand foot, and four or five thousand horse; but then they were all brave men; were well disciplined, and inured to fatigue; had made several campaigns under Philip; and were each of them, in case of necessity capable of commanding. Most of the officers were near threescore years of age; and when they were either assembled, or drawn up at the head of a camp, they had the air of a venerable senate. Parmenio commanded the infantry. Philotas, his son, had eighteen hundred horse under him; and Callas, the same number of Thessalian cavalry. The rest of the horse, who were composed of natives of the several states of Greece, and amounted to six hundred, had their particular commander. The Thracians and Pæonians, who were always in front, were headed by Cassander. Alexander began his route along the lake Circinum towards Amphipolis; crossed the river Stryman, near its mouth; afterwards the Hebrus, and arrived at Sestos after twenty days march. He
then

then commanded Parmenio to cross over from Sestos to Abydos, with all the horse and part of the foot;—which he accordingly did by the assistance of an hundred and three score gallies, and several flat-bottomed vessels. As for Alexander, he went from Eleontum to the port of the Achaians, himself steering his own galley; and being got to the middle of the Hellespont, he sacrificed a bull to Neptune and the Nereides; and made effusions in the sea from a golden cup. It is also related, that after having thrown a javelin at the land, as thereby to take possession of it, he landed first in Asia; and leaping from the ship completely armed, and in the highest transports of joy, he erected altars on the shore to Jupiter, to Minerva, and to Hercules, for having favoured him with so propitious a descent. He had done the same at his leaving Europe.

He depended so entirely on the happy success of his arms, and the rich spoils he should find in Asia, that he had made very little provision for so great an expedition; persuaded that war when carried on successfully, would supply all things necessary for war.

He had but seventy talents in money (seventy thousand crowns) to pay his army, and only a month's provision; but his soldiers were inspired with so much courage and security, that they fancied they marched not to precarious war, but certain victory.

Being arrived at the city of Lampsacus, which he was determined to destroy, in order to punish the rebellion of its inhabitants, Aneximenes, a native of that place, came to him. This man, who was a famous historian, had been very intimate with Philip his father; and Alexander himself had a great esteem for him, having been his pupil. The king suspecting

fufpecting the bufinefs he was come t
beforehand with him, fwore, in exprefs t
would never grant his requeft. The fa
to defire of you, fays Anaximenes, is, tha
deftroy Lampfacus. By this witty eva
torian faved his country.

From thence Alexander arrived at
he paid great honours to the manes of *l*
caufed games to be celebrated round his
admired and envied the double felicity
nowned Grecian, in having found during
a faithful friend in Patroclus; and aftei
herald in Homer, worthy the greatnef
ploits.

At laft Alexander arrived on the t
Granicus, a river of Phrygia. The Sat
puty-lieutenants, waited his coming on t
of it, firmly refolved to difpute the paffa
Their army confifted of one hundred th
and upwards of ten thoufand horfe. N
was a Rhodian, and commanded und
the coaft of Afia, had advifed the general
ture a battle; but to lay wafte the plai
the cities, thereby to ftarve Alexandei
oblige him to return back into Europ
was the beft of all Darius's generals, a
the principal agent in his victories. Bi
Phrygian Satrap, oppofed the opinion
and protefted he would never fuffer the
make fuch havoc in the territories h
This ill council prevailed over that of
(Memnon) whom the Perfians, to thei
dice, fufpected of a defign to protract th
that means make himfelf neceffary to D

Alexander, in the mean time, marched on at the head of his heavy armed infantry, drawn up in two lines, with the cavalry in the wings: the baggage followed in the rear. Being arrived upon the banks of the Granicus, Parmenio advised him to encamp there in battle-array, in order that his forces might have time to rest themselves, and not to pass the river till very early next morning, because the enemy would then be less able to prevent him. He added, that it would be too dangerous to attempt crossing a river in sight of an enemy, especially as that before them was deep, and its banks very craggy; so that the Persian cavalry, who waited their coming in battle-array, on the other side, might easily defeat them before they were drawn up. That besides the loss which would be sustained on this occasion, this enterprise, in case it should prove unsuccessful, would be of dangerous consequence to their future affairs; the fame and glory of arms depending on the first actions.

However, these reasons were not able to make the least impression on Alexander, who declared, that it would be a shame, should he, after crossing the Hellespont, suffer his progress to be retarded by a rivulet, for so he called the Granicus out of contempt; that they ought to take advantage of the terrour, which the suddenness of his arrival, and the boldness of his attempt, had spread among the Persians; and answer the high opinion the world conceived of his courage, and the valour of the Macedonians. The enemy's horse, which was very numerous, lined the whole shore, and formed a large front, in order to oppose Alexander, wherever he should endeavour to pass, and the foot which consisted chiefly of Greeks,

in

in Darius's service, was posted behind, upon an easy ascent.

The two armies continued a long time in sight of each other, on the banks of the river, as if dreading the event. The Persians waited till the Macedonians should enter the river, in order to charge them to advantage upon their landing; and the latter seemed to be making choice of a place proper for crossing, and to survey the countenance of their enemies. Upon this, Alexander having ordered his horse to be brought, commanded the noblemen of the court to follow him, and behave gallantly. He himself commanded the right wing, and Parmenio the left. The king first caused a strong detachment to march into the river, himself following it with the rest of the forces. He made Parmenio advance afterwards with the left wing. He himself led on the right wing into the river, followed by the rest of the troops; the trumpet sounding, and the whole army raising cries of joy.

The Persians, seeing this detachment advance forward, began to let fly their arrows, and march to a place where the declivity was not so great, in order to keep the Macedonians from landing. But now the horse engaged with great fury; one part endeavouring to land, and the other striving to prevent them. The Macedonians, whose cavalry was vastly inferior in number, besides the advantage of ground, were wounded with darts that were shot from the eminence; not to mention that the flower of the Persian horse were drawn together in this place; and that Memnon, in concert with his sons, commanded there. The Macedonians therefore at first gave ground, after having lost their first ranks, made a vigorous defence. Alexander, who had followed them close, and reinforced them with his best troops, heads them himself, animates them by his presence, pushes the Persians, and routs them; upon which the whole army follow after, cross the river, and attack the enemy on all sides.

Alexander first charged the thickest part of the enemy's horse, in which the generals fought. He himself was particularly conspicuous by his shield, and the plume of feathers that overshadowed his helmet, on the two sides of which there rose two wings as it were, of a great length, and so vastly white, that they dazzled the eyes of the beholder. The charge was very furious about his person; and though only horse engaged, they fought like foot, man to man, without giving way on either side; every one striving to repulse his adversary, and gain ground of him. Spithrobates, lieutenant-governor of Ionia, and son-in-law to Darius, distinguished himself above the rest of the generals by his superiour bravery. Being surrounded by forty Persian lords, all of them his relations, of experienced valour, and who never moved from his side, he carried terror wherever he moved. Alexander observing in how gallant a manner he signalised himself, clapped spurs to his horse, and advanced towards him. Immediately they engage, and each having thrown a javelin, wounded the other slightly. Spithrobates falls furiously sword in hand upon Alexander, who being prepared for him, thrusts his pike into his face, and laid him dead at his feet. At that very moment, Rosaces, brother to that nobleman, charging him on that side, gives him so furious a blow on the head with his battle-axe, that he beat off his plume,

plume, but went no deeper than the hair. As he was going to repeat his blow on the head, which now appeared through his fractured helmet, Clitus cuts off Rofaces' hand with one stroke of his scimetar, and by that means saved his sovereign's life. The danger to which Alexander had been exposed, greatly animated the courage of his soldiers, who now perform wonders. The Persians in the centre of the horse, upon whom the light-armed troops, who had been posted in the intervals of the horse, poured a perpetual discharge of darts; being unable to sustain any longer the attack of the Macedonians, who struck them all in the face, the two wings were immediately broke and put to flight. Alexander did not pursue them long, but turned about immediately to charge the foot.

Thefe, says the historian, at first stood their ground, which was owing to the surprise they were seized with, rather than bravery. But when they saw themselves attacked at the same time by the cavalry, and the Macedonian phalanx, which had crossed the river, and that the battalions were now engaged; those of the Persians did not make either a long or a vigorous resistance, and were soon put to flight, the Grecian infantry in Darius' service excepted. This body of foot retiring to a hill, demanded a promise from Alexander to let them march away unmolested; but following the dictates of passion, rather than those of reason, he rushed into the midst of this body of foot, and presently lost his horse (not Bucephalus) who was killed with the thrust of a sword. The battle was so hot round him, that most of the Macedonians, who lost their lives on this occasion, fell here; for they fought against a body of men who

were

were well difciplined, had been inured to war, and fought in defpair. They were all cut to pieces, two thoufand excepted, who were taken prifoners.

A great number of the chief Perfian commanders lay dead on the fpot. Arfites fled into Phrygia, where it is faid he laid violent hands upon himfelf, for having been the caufe that the battle was fought. Twenty thoufand foot, and two thoufand five hundred horfe, were killed in this engagement, on the fide of the Barbarians; and of the Macedonians, twenty-five of the royal horfe were killed at the firſt attack. Alexander ordered Lyfippus to make their ftatues in brafs, all which were fet up in a city of Macedon called Dia, in honour of them, from whence they were many years after carried to Rome by Q. Metellus. About three fcore of the other horfe were killed; and near thirty foot, who, the next day, were all laid, with their arms and equipage, in one grave; and the king granted an exemption to their fathers and children from every kind of tribute and fervice.

He alfo took the utmoft care of the wounded, vifited them, and faw their wounds dreffed. He enquired very particularly into their adventures, and permitted every one of them to relate his actions in the battle, and boaft his bravery. He alfo granted the rites of fepulture to the grandees of Perfia, and did not even refufe it to fuch Greeks as died in the Perfian fervice; but all thofe whom he took prifoners he laid in chains, and fent them to work as flaves in Macedonia, for having fought under the Barbarian ftandards againft their country, contrary to the exprefs prohibition made by Greece upon that head.

Alexander

Alexander made it his duty and pleasure to share the honour of his victory with the Greeks; and sent particularly to the Athenians three hundred shields, being part of the plunder taken from the enemy; and caused the following inscription to be inscribed on the rest of the spoils: 'Alexander, son of Philip, with the Greeks (the Lacedæmonians excepted) gained these spoils from the Barbarians, who inhabit Asia.' The greatest part of the gold and silver plate, the purple carpets, and other furniture of the Persian luxury, he sent to his mother.

SECT. IV. *Alexander conquers the greatest part of Asia-Minor. He falls sick of a mortal distemper, occasioned by bathing in the river Sydnus. Philip the physician cures him in a few days. Alexander ... the streights of Cilicia. Darius advances at the same time. The bold and free answer of Caridemus to that prince, which costs him his life. Description of Darius' march.*

(a) THE success of the battle of Granicus had all the happy consequences that could naturally be expected from it. Sardis, which was in a manner the bulwark of the Barbarian empire on the side next the sea, surrendered to Alexander, who thereupon gave the citizens their liberty, and permitted them to live after their own laws. Four days after he arrived at Ephesus, carrying with him those who had been banished from thence for being his adherents, and restored its popular form of government.

He

(a) A. M. 3671. Ant. J. C. 333.

He assigned to the temple of Diana the tributes which were paid to the kings of Persia. He offered a great number of sacrifices to that goddess; solemnised her mysteries with the utmost pomp, and conducted the ceremony with his whole army drawn up in battle array. The Ephesians had begun to rebuild the temple of Diana, which had been burned the night of Alexander's birth, and the work was now very forward. Dinocrates, a famous architect, who superintended this edifice, was employed by 'this king to build Alexandria in Egypt. Alexander offered to pay the Ephesians all the expences they had already been at, and to furnish the remainder, provided they would inscribe the temple only with his name; the inhabitants of Ephesus not being willing to consent to it, and however afraid to refuse him that honour openly, had recourse to an artful flattery for an evasion. They told him, that it was inconsistent for one god to erect monuments to another. Before he left Ephesus, the deputies of the cities of Trallis and Magnesia, waited upon him with the keys of those places.

He afterwards marched to Miletus, which city, flattered with the hope of a sudden and powerful support, shut their gates against him: and indeed the Persian fleet, which was very considerable, made a shew as if it would succour that city; but after having made several fruitless attempts to engage that of the enemy, it was forced to sail away. Memnon had shut himself up in this fortress, with a great number of his soldiers, who had escaped from the battle, and was determined to make a good defence. Alexander, who would not lose a moments time, attacked it and planted scaling ladders on all sides.

The scalado was carried on with great vigour, and opposed with no less intrepidity, though Alexander sent fresh troops to relieve one another without the least intermission; and this lasted several days. At last, finding his soldiers were every where repulsed, and that the city was provided with every thing for a long siege, he planted all his machines against it, made a great number of breaches, and whenever these were attacked, a new scalado was attempted. The besieged after sustaining all these efforts with prodigious bravery, capitulated for fear of being taken by storm. Alexander treated all the Milesians with the utmost humanity, and sold all the foreigners who were found in it. The historians do not make any mention of Memnon, but we may reasonably suppose that he marched out with the garrison.

Alexander, seeing that the enemy's fleet was sailed away, resolved to lay up his own, the expence of it being too great, not to mention that he wanted money for things of greater importance. Some historians are even of opinion, that as he was upon the point of coming to a battle with Darius, which was to determine the fate of the two empires, he was resolved to deprive his soldiers of all hopes of retreat, and to leave them no other resource than that of victory. He, therefore, retained such vessels only of his fleet, as were absolutely necessary for transporting the military engines, and a small number of other gallies.

After possessing himself of Miletus, he marched into Caria, in order to lay siege to Halicarnassus. This city was of prodigious difficult access from its happy situation, and had been strongly fortified. Besides Memnon, the ablest as well as the most valiant

liant of all Darius' commanders, had got into it with a body of choice soldiers, with design to signalize his courage and fidelity for his sovereign. He accordingly made a very noble defence, in which he was seconded by Ephialtes, another general of great merit. Whatever could be expected from the most intrepid bravery, and the most consummate knowledge in the science of war, was conspicuous on this occasion. After the besiegers had, with incredible labour, filled up part of the ditches, and brought their engines near the walls, they had the grief to see their works demolished in an instant, and their engines set on fire, by the frequent vigorous sallies of the besieged. After beating down part of a wall with their battering rams, they were astonished to see a new one behind it; which was so sudden, that it seemed to rise out of the ground. The attack of these walls, which were built in a semi-circular form, destroyed a prodigious number of men; because the besieged, from the top of the towers that were raised on the several sides, took the enemy in flank. It was evidently seen at this siege, that the strongest fortifications of a city are the valour and courage of its defenders. The siege was held out so long, and attended with such surprising difficulties, as would have discouraged any warrior but an Alexander; yet his troops were animated by the view of dangers, and their patience was at last successful. Memnon finding it impossible for him to hold out any longer, was forced to abandon the city. As the sea was open to him, after having put a strong garrison into the citadel, which was well stored with provisions, he took with him the surviving inhabitants, with all their riches, and conveyed them into the island of Cos, which was not

far

far from Halicarnaſſus. Alexander did not think proper to beſiege the citadel, it being of little importance after the city was deſtroyed, which he demoliſhed to the very foundations. He left it, after having encompaſſed it with ſtrong walls, and left ſome good troops in the country.

After the death of Artemiſia, queen of Caria, Idrieus her brother reigned in her ſtead. The ſceptre devolved upon Ada, ſiſter and wife of Idrieus, according to the cuſtom of the country; but ſhe was dethroned by Pexodorus, to whom ſucceeded by Darius' command, Orontobates, his ſon in law. Ada, was however ſtill poſſeſſed of a fortreſs called Alinda, the keys of which ſhe had carried to Alexander, the inſtant ſhe heard of his arrival in Caria, and had adopted him for her ſon. The king was ſo far from contemning this honour, that he left her the quiet poſſeſſion of her own city; and, after having taken Halicarnaſſus, as he by that means was maſter of the whole country, he reſtored the government of it to Ada.

This lady, as a teſtimony of the deep ſenſe ſhe had of the favours received from Alexander, ſent him every day meats dreſſed in the moſt exquiſite manner; delicious pies of all ſorts, and the moſt excellent cooks of every kind. Alexander anſwered the queen on this occaſion—" That all this train
" was of no ſervice to him, for that he was poſſeſſed
" of much better cooks, whom Leonidas his go-
" vernor had given him; one of whom prepared
" him a good dinner, and that was by walking a
" great deal in the morning very early; and the
" other prepared him an excellent ſupper, and that
" was dining very moderately."

Several

Several kings of Asia-Minor submitted voluntarily to Alexander. Mithridates king of Pontus was one of these, who afterwards adhered to this prince, and followed him in his expeditions. He was son to Ariobarzanes, governor of Phrygia, and king of Pontus. He is computed to be the sixteenth king from Artabazus, who is considered as the founder of this kingdom, of which he was put in possession by Darius. Alexander, before he went into winter quarters, permitted all such of his soldiers, as had married that year, to return into Macedonia, there to spend the winter with their wives, upon condition that they would return in the spring. He appointed three officers to march with them thither and back again.

The next year Alexander began the campaign very early. He had debated, whether it would be proper for him to march directly against Darius, or should first subdue the rest of the maritime provinces. The latter opinion appeared the safest, since he thereby would not be molested by such nations as he should leave behind him. This progress was a little interrupted at first. Near Phaselis, a city situated between Lycia and Pamphylia, is a defile along the sea shore, which is always dry at low water, so that travellers may pass it at that time; but when the sea rises, it is all under water. As it was now winter, Alexander, whom nothing could daunt, was desirous of passing it before the waters fell. His forces were, therefore obliged to march a whole day in the water, which came up to their waist. Some historians, purely to embellish this incident, relate that the sea, by the divine command, had submitted spontaneously to Alexander, and had opened a way to him, contrary

trary to the usual course of nature; among these writers is Quintus Curtius; but the falsity of this, Alexander himself has refuted. For Plutarch relates, that he wrote only as follows in one of his letters, That when he left the city of Phaselis, he marched on foot through the pass of the mountain called Climax: and it is very well known, that this prince, who was vastly fond of the marvellous, never let slip any opportunity of persuading the people, that the gods protected him in a very singular manner.

During his being in the neighbourhood of Phaselis, he discovered a conspiracy which was carrying on by Alexander, son of Eropus, whom he had a little before appointed general of the Thessalian cavalry, in the room of Calas, whom he had made governor of a province. Darius, upon the receipt of a letter which this traitor had sent him, promised him a reward of a thousand * talents of gold with the kingdom of Macedonia, in case he could murder Alexander; believing this was not paying too dear for a crime, which would rid him of so formidable an enemy. The messenger who carried the kings' answer being seized, made a full confession, by which means the traitor was brought to condign punishment.

Alexander after having settled affairs in Cilicia and Pamphylia, marched his army to Celænæ, a city of Phrygia, watered by the river Marsyas, which the fiction of the poets have made so famous. He summoned the garrison of the citadel, whither the inhabitants were retired, to surrender; but these believing it impregnable, answered haughtily, that they would first die. However, finding the attack carried

* About one million five hundred thousand pounds sterling.

ried on with great vigour, they defired a truce of fixty days, at the expiration of which they promifed to open their gates, in cafe they were not fuccoured : and accordingly no aid arriving, they furrendered themfelves upon the day fixed.

From thence the king marched into Phrygia, the capital of which was called Gordion, the ancient and famous refidence of king Midas, fituated on the river Sangarius. Having taken the city, he was defirous of feeing the famous chariot to which the Gordian knot was tied. This knot, which faftened the yoke to the beam, was tied with fo much art, and the ftrings were twifted in fo wonderful a manner, that it was impoffible to difcover where it begun or ended. According to an ancient tradition of the country, an oracle had foretold, that the man who could untie it fhould poffefs the empire of Afia. Now Alexander was firmly perfuaded this promife related to himfelf; after many fruitlefs trials, he cried, It is no matter which way it be untied, and thereupon cut it with his fword, and by that means, either eluded or fulfilled the oracle.

In the mean time Darius was fetting every engine at work, in order to make a vigorous defence. Memnon the Rhodian advifed him to carry the war into Macedonia. Which council feemed the moft proper to extricate him from the prefent danger; for the Lacedæmonians, and feveral other Greek nations, who had no affection for the Macedonians, would have been ready to join him; by which means Alexander muft have been forced to leave Afia, and return fuddenly over fea, to defend his own country. Darius approved this counfel, and, having determined to follow it, charged Memnon to put it into execution.

Accordingly

Accordingly he was declared admiral of the fleet, and captain-general of all the forces designed for that expedition.

That prince could not possibly have made a better choice. Memnon was the ablest general in his service, and had fought a great many years under the Persian standards with the utmost fidelity. Had his advice been taken, the battle of Granicus had not been fought. He did not abandon his masters' interests after that misfortune, but had assembled the scattered remains of the army, and immediately went first to Miletus, from thence to Halicarnassus, and lastly into the island of Cos, where he was when he received his new commission. This place was the rendezvous of the fleet; and Memnon was now meditating wholly upon the manner how to put his design in execution. He made himself master of the island of Chios, and all Lesbos, the city of Mitilene excepted. From thence he was preparing to pass over into Euboea, and to make Greece and Macedonia the seat of the war, but died before Mitylene, which city he had been forced to besiege. The loss of Memnon frustrated the execution of the plan he had formed; for Darius not having one general in his army who was able to supply Memnon's place, abandoned entirely the only enterprise which could have saved his empire. His whole refuge, therefore, now lay in the armies of the East. Darius, dissatisfied with all his generals, resolved to command in person, and appointed Babylon for the rendezvous of his army; whereupon being mustered, they were found to be about four, five, or six hundred thousand men, for historians differ very much on this head.

Alexander

Alexander having left Gordion, marched into Paphlagonia and Cappadocia, which he subdued. It was there he heard of Memnon's death, the news whereof confirmed him in the resolution he had taken of marching immediately into the provinces of Upper Asia. Accordingly he advanced by hasty marches into Cilicia, and arrived into the country called Cyrus' camp. From thence Alexander marched his whole army to the city of Tarsus, where it arrived the instant the Persians were setting fire to that place, to prevent his plundering the great riches of so flourishing a city. But Parmenio, whom the king had sent thither with a detachment of horse, arrived very seasonably to stop the progress of the fire, and marched into the city, which he saved; the Barbarians having fled the moment they heard of his arrival.

Through this city the Cydnus runs, a river remarkable for the beauty of its waters, which are vastly limpid; but at the same time excessively cold, because of the tufted trees with which its banks are over-shadowed. It was now about the end of summer, which is excessively hot in Cilicia, and in the hottest part of the day, when the king, who was quite covered with sweat and dirt, arriving on its banks, had a mind to bathe in that river, invited by the beauty and clearness of the stream. However, the instant he plunged into it, he was seized with so violent a shivering, that all the standers-by fancied he was dying. Upon this he was carried to his tent, after fainting away. The news of this sad disaster threw the whole army into the utmost consternation.

At last the king recovered his senses by degrees, and began to know the persons who stood round him;

him; but he was more indisposed in mind than body, for news was brought that Darius might soon arrive. Alexander bewailed perpetually his hard fate, in being thus exposed naked and defenceless to his enemy, and robbed of so noble a victory, since he was now reduced to the melancholy condition of dying obscurely in his tent, and far from having attained the glory he had promised himself. Having ordered his confidents and physicians to come into his tent "You see
" (says he) my friends, the sad extremity to which
" fortune reduces me. Methinks I already hear the
" sound of the enemy's arms, and see Darius advan-
" cing. He undoubtedly held intelligence with my
" evil genius * when he wrote letters to his lieute-
" nants in so lofty and contemptous a strain; how-
" ever, he shall not obtain his desire, provided such
" a cure as I want is attempted. The present con-
" dition of my affairs will not admit of slow reme-
" dies or fearful physicians. A speedy death is
" more eligible to me than a slow cure. In case the
" physicians think to do me any good, they are to
" know that I do not so much wish to live as to
" fight."

This sudden impatience of the king spread an universal alarm. The physicians, who were sensible they should be answerable for the event, did not dare to hazard violent and extraordinary remedies; especially as Darius had published, that he would reward with a thousand talents (about 145,000 l. sterling) the man who should kill Alexander. However

---

* Dari , who imagined himself sure of overcoming Alexander, had wrote to his lieutenants, that they should chastise this young fool; and after clothing him in purple out of derision, should send him bound hand and foot to the court.

ever, Philip an Arcanian, one of his phyſicians, who had always attended upon him from his youth, loved him with the utmoſt tenderneſs, not only as his ſovereign but his child; raiſing himſelf (merely out of affection to Alexander) above all prudential conſiderations, offered to give him a doſe; which, though not very violent, would nevertheleſs be ſpeedy in its effects; and deſired three days to prepare it. At this propoſal every one trembled, but him only whom it moſt concerned; Alexander being afflicted upon no other account, than becauſe it would keep him three days from appearing at the head of his army.

Whilſt theſe things were doing, Alexander received a letter from Parmenio, who was left behind in Capadocia, in whom Alexander put greater confidence than in any other of his courtiers; the purport of which was, to bid him beware of Philip, for that Darius had bribed him, by the promiſe of a thouſand talents, and his ſiſter in marriage. This letter gave him great uneaſineſs, for he was now at full leiſure to weigh all the reaſons he might have to hope or to fear. But the confidence in a phyſician, whoſe ſincere attachment and fidelity he had proved from his infancy, ſoon prevailed, and removed all his doubts. Upon this, he folded up the letter, and put it under his bolſter, without acquainting any one with the contents of it.

The day being come, Philip enters the tent with his medicine, when Alexander taking the letter from under the bolſter, gives it Philip to read. At the ſame time he takes the cup and fixing his eyes on the phyſician, ſwallows the draught without the leaſt heſitation, or without diſcovering the leaſt ſuſpicion

or

or uneasiness. Philip, as he perused the letter, had shewed greater signs of indignation than of fear or surprise; and throwing himself upon the king's bed —Royal sir (says he) your recovery will soon clear me of the guilt of parricide with which I am charged. The only favour I beg is, that you would be easy in your own mind; and suffer the draught to operate, and not regard the intelligence you have received from servants, who indeed have shewn their zeal for your welfare; which zeal, however, is very indiscreet and unseasonable. These words did not only revive the king, but filled him with hope and joy; so taking Philip by the hand, Be yourself (says he to him) for I believe you are disquieted upon a double account; first for my recovery, and secondly for your own justification.

In the mean time, the physic worked so violently, that the accidents which attended it, strengthened Parmenio's accusation; for the king lost his speech, and was seized with such strong fainting fits, that he had hardly any pulse left, or the least symptoms of life. Philip employed all the powers of physic to recover him, and in every lucid interval, diverted him with agreeable subjects; discoursing one moment about his mother and sisters, and another about the mighty victory which was advancing, with hasty steps, to crown his past triumphs. At last the physician's art having gained the ascendant, and diffused through every vein a salutary and vivifick virtue; his mind began to resume its former vigour, and afterwards his body, much sooner than had been expected. Three days after he shewed himself to the army, who were never satisfied with gazing upon him, and could scarce believe their eyes; so much the greatness of the danger had surprised and dejected them. No caresses were enough for the physician; every one embracing him with the utmost tenderness, and returning him thanks as a God who had saved the life of their sovereign.

During this interval, Darius was on his march, full of a vain security in the infinite number of his troops, and forming a judgment of the two armies merely from their disparity in that point. The plains of Assyria, in which he was encamped, gave him an opportunity of extending his horse as he pleased, and of taking the advantage which the great difference between the number of soldiers in each army gave him; but instead of this, he resolves to march to narrow passes, where his cavalry and the multitude of his troops, so far from doing him any service, would only incumber one another; and accordingly he advances towards the enemy, for whom he should have waited, and runs visibly to his own destruction. Nevertheless, the grandees of his court, whose custom it was to flatter and applaud his every action, congratulated him beforehand on the victory he would soon obtain, as if it had been certain and inevitable. There was at that time, in the army of Darius, one Caridemus, an Athenian, a man of great experience in war, who persona ly hated Alexander, for having caused him to be banished from Athens. Darius turning to this Athenian, asked, whether he believed him powerful enough to defeat his enemy. Caridemus, who had been brought up in the bosom of liberty, and forgetting that he was in a country of slavery, where to oppose the inclinations of a prince is of the most dangerous consequence, replied as follows: " Possibly, sir, you may not be pleased with
" my

" my telling you the truth; but in case I do not do
" it now, it will be too late hereafter. This mighty
" parade of war, this prodigious number of men
" which has drained all the east, might indeed be
" formidable to your neighbours. Gold and pur-
" ple shine in every part of your army, which is so
" prodigiously splendid, that those who have not
" seen it, could never form an idea of its magnifi-
" cence. But the soldiers who compose the Ma e-
" donian army, terrible to behold, and bristling in
" every part with arms, do not amuse their es
" with such idle show. Their only care is to disci-
" pline, in a regular manner, their battalions, and to
" cover themselves close with their bucklers and
" pikes. Their phalanx is a body of infantry, which
" engages without flinching; and keeps so close in
" their ranks, that the soldiers and their arms form a
" kind of impenetrable work. In a word, every sin-
" gle man among them, the officers as well soldiers,
" are so well trained up, so attentive to the com-
" mand of their leaders, that whither they are to af-
" semble under their standards, to turn to the right
" or left, to double their ranks, and face about to the
" enemy on all sides, at the least signal they make
" every motion and evolution of the art of war.
" But that you may be persuaded, these Macedoni-
" ans were not invited hither, from the hopes of gain-
" ing gold and silver; know, that this excellent dis-
" cipline has subsisted hitherto by the sole aid and
" precepts of poverty. Are they hungry? they sa-
" tisfy their appetite with any kind of food. Are
" they weary? they repose themselves on the bare
" ground, and in the day time are always upon their
" feet. Do you fancy that the Thessalian cavalry,
and

" and that of Acarnania and Ætolia, who all are
" armed cap-a-pee, are to be repulsed by stones
" hurled from slings, and with sticks burnt at the
" ends ? such troops as are like themselves, will be
" able to check their career ; and succours must be
" procured from their country, to oppose their bra-
" very and experience. Send therefore thither all
" the useless gold and silver which I see here, and
" purchase formidable soldiers." But Darius, not
having strength of mind sufficient for this, gives orders
for dragging to execution a man who had fled to him
for protection, was at that time his guest, and gave
him at that time the best counsel that could have
been proposed to him. However, as this cruel treatment could not silence Ceridemus, he cried aloud,
with his usual freedom ; " My avenger is at hand,
" the very man in opposition, to whom I gave you
" council, and he will soon punish you for despising
" it. As for you, Darius, in whom sovereign pow-
" er has wrought so sudden a change, you will teach
" posterity, that when once men abandon themselves
" to the delusion of fortune, she erases from their
" minds all the seeds of goodness implanted in them
" by nature." Darius soon repented his having put
to death so valuable a person ; and experienced, but
too late, the truth of all he had told him.

The king advanced with his troops towards the
Euphrates. It was a custom long used by the Persians, never to set out upon a march til after sunrise,
at which time the trumpet was sounded for that purpose from the king's tent. Over this tent was exhibited to the view of the whole army, the image of
the sun set in cryſtal. The order they observed in
their march was this.

First,

First, they carried silver altars, on which there lay fire, called by them sacred and eternal; and these were followed by the Magi, singing hymns after the manner of their country. They were accompanied by three hundred and sixty-five youths (agreeable to the number of days in a year) clothed in purple robes. Afterwards came a chariot consecrated to Jupiter, drawn by white horses, and followed 'y a courser of a prodigious size, to whom they g⁻ the name of the sun's horse; and the equerr were dressed in white, each having a golden rod in his hand.

Ten chariots, adorned with sculptures in gold and silver, followed after. Then marched a body of horse composed of twelve nations, whose manners and customs were various, and all armed in a different manner. Next advanced those whom the Persians called the immortals, amounting to ten thousand, who surpassed the rest of the Barbarians in the sumptuousness of their apparel. They all wore golden collars, were clothed in robes of gold tissue, with surtouts (having sleeves to them) quite covered with precious stones.

Thirty paces from them, followed those called the kings cousins or * relations, to the number of fifteen thousand, in habits resembling very much those of women, and more remarkable for the vain pomp of their dress than the glitter of their arms.

Those called the Doryphori (these were guards who carried half a pike) came after; they carried the kings cloak, and walked before his chariot, in which he seemed to sit as on a high throne. This chariot was

enriched

---

* *This was a title of dignity. Possibly a great number of the kings relations were in this body.*

enriched on both sides with images of all the gods in gold and silver; and from the middle of the yoke, which was covered with jewels, rose two statues a cubit in height, the one representing war, the other peace, having a golden eagle between them, with wings extended, as ready to take its flight.

But nothing could equal the magnificence of the king. He was clothed in a vest of purple, striped with silver, and over it a long robe glittering all over with gold and precious stones, that represented two falcons rushing from the clouds, and pecking at one another. Around his waist he wore a golden girdle, after the manner of women, whence his scymitar hung, the scabbard of which flamed all over with gems, on his head he wore a tiara or mitre, round which was a fillet of blue mixed with white.

On each side of him walked two hundred of his nearest relations, followed by ten thousand pikemen, whose pikes were adorned with silver, and tipped with gold; and lastly, thirty thousand infantry, who composed the rear-guard. These were followed by the kings horses (four hundred in number) all which were led.

About one hundred and twenty paces from thence, came Sysigambis, Darius's mother, seated on a chariot, and his consort on another, with the several female attendants of both queens riding on horseback. Afterwards came fifteen large chariots, in which were the king's children, and those who had the care of their education, with a band of eunuchs, who are to this day in great esteem with those nations. Then marched the concubines, to the number of three hundred and sixty, in the equipage of queens, followed by six hundred mules, and three hundred camels, which carried the kings treasure, and were guarded by a body of archers.

After these came the wives of the crown-officers, and of the greatest lords of the court; then the sutlers, and servants of the army, seated also in chariots.

In the rear were a body of light-armed troops, with their commanders, who closed the whole march.

Would not the reader believe he had been reading the description of a tournament, not the march of an army? could he imagine that princes of the least reason would have been so stupid, as to incorporate with their forces so cumbersome a train of women, princesses, concubines, eunuchs, and domesticks of both sexes. But the custom of the country was reason sufficient for Darius.

SECT. V. *Alexander gains a famous victory over Darius, near the city of Issus. The consequences of that victory.*

(f) FOR the clearer understanding of Alexander's march, and that of Darius, and the better fixing the situation of the spot where the second battle was fought, we must distinguish three straits or passes. The first of these is immediately at the descent from mount Taurus, in the way to the city of Tarsus, through which Alexander marched from Cappadocia into Cilicia. The second is the pass of Cilicia or Syria, leading from Cilicia into Syria; and the third is the pass of Amanus, so called from that mountain. This pass, which leads into Cilicia from Assyria, is much higher than the pass of Syria, northward.

Alexander

(f) A. M. 3672. Ant. J. C. 332.

Alexander had detached Parmenio with part of the army to seize the pafs of Syria, in order to secure it for his march. As for himfelf, after marching from Tarfus, he arrived the next day at Anchiala, a city which Sardinapalus is faid to have built. His tomb was ftill to be feen in that city with this infcription, Sardanapalus built Anchiala and Tarfus in one day: Go paffenger, eat, drink, and rejoice, for the reft is nothing. From hence he came to Soloe where he offered facrifices to Æfculapius, in gratitude for the recovery of his health. Alexander himfelf headed the ceremony with lighted tapers, followed by the whole army, and he there folemnized games; after which he returned to Tarfus. Having commanded Philotas to march the cavalry through the plains of Aleius, towards the river Pyramus, he himfelf went with the infantry and his life-guard to Magarfus, whence he arrived at Malles, and afterwards at Caftabala. Advice had been brought him, that Darius, with his whole army, was encamped at Sochus in Affyria, two days journey from Cilicia. There Alexander held a council of war upon that news; when all his generals and officers entreating him to march towards Darius, he fet out the next day to give him battle. Parmenio had taken the little city of Iffus, and, after poffeffing himfelf of the pafs of Syria, had left a body of forces to fecure it. The king left the fick in Iffus, marched his whole army through the pafs, and encamped near the city of Myriandrus, where the badnefs of the weather obliged him to halt.

In the mean time, Darius was in the plains of Affyria, of great extent. The Grecian commanders who were in his fervice, and formed the chief ftrength
of

of his army, advised him to wait there the coming-up of the enemy. For, besides that this spot was open on all sides, and very advantageous for his horse, it was spacious enough to contain his vastly numerous host, with all the baggage and other things belonging to the army. However, if he should not approve of their council, they then advised him to separate this multitude, and select such only as were the flower of his troops; and consequently not venture his whole army upon a single battle, which perhaps might be decisive. However, the courtiers, with whom the courts of monarchs forever abound, called these Greeks an unfaithful nation, and venal wretches; and hinted to Darius, that the only motive of their counselling the king to divide his troops was, that, after they should once be separated from the rest, they might have an easier opportunity of delivering up into the enemies hands whatever might be in their power; but that the safest way would be, to surround them with the whole army, and cut them to pieces, as an illustrious example of the punishment due to traitors. This proposal was vastly shocking to Darius, who was naturally of a mild and humane disposition. He therefore answered. " That he was far from ever designing
" to commit so horrible a crime; that should he be
" guilty of it, no nation would afterwards give the
" least credit to his promises; that no man would
" ever venture to give his opinion, if it were attend-
" ed with such danger, a circumstance that would
" be of the most fatal consequences to princes."
He then thanked the Greeks for their zeal and good will, and condescended to lay before th.. he reasons which prompted him not to follow their ad

Darius,

Darius, having sent his treasure with his most precious moveables to Damascus, a city of Syria, under a small convoy, marched the main body of his army towards Cilicia, and entered it by the pass of Amanus, which lies far above the passes of Syria. His queen and mother, with the princesses his daughters, and the little prince his son, followed the army according to the custom of the Persians, but were in the camp during the battle. When he had advanced a little way into Cilicia (from east, westward) he turned short towards Issus, not knowing that Alexander was behind; for he had been assured that this prince fled before him, and was retired in great disorder into Syria; and therefore Darius was now considering how he might best pursue him. He barbarously put to death all the sick who were then in the city of Issus, a few soldiers excepted, whom he dismissed, after making them view every part of his camp, in order that they might be spectators of the prodigious multitude of his forces. These soldiers accordingly brought Alexander word of Darius' approach, which he could scarcely believe, from its great improbability, though there was nothing he desired more earnestly. But he himself was soon an eye-witness to the truth of it, upon which he began to think seriously of preparing for battle.

Alexander fearing, as the Barbarians were so numerous, that they would attack him in his camp, fortified it with ditches and palisadoes, discovering an incredible joy to see his desire fulfilled, which was, to engage in those passes; and indeed, this spot of ground, which was but wide enough for a small army to act and move at liberty in, reduced, in some measure, the two armies to an equality. By this
F means

means the Macedonians had space sufficient to employ their whole army, whereas the Persians had not room for the twentieth part of theirs.

Nevertheless, Alexander felt some emotion when he saw that he was going to hazard all at one blow. The more fortune had favoured him hitherto, the more he now dreaded her frowns; the moment approaching which was to determine his fate; but although he was uncertain with regard to the victory, he at least hoped to die gloriously, and like Alexander; he was also determined his troops should read nothing but intrepidity in the countenance of their commander.

Having made his soldiers refresh themselves, and ordered them to be ready for the third watch of the night, which began at twelve, he went to the top of a mountain, and there, by torch-light, sacrificed after the manner of his country, to the gods of the place. As soon as the signal was given, his army, which was ready to march and fight, being commanded to make greater speed, arrived by day-break at the several posts assigned them, but now the couriers bringing word that Darius was not above thirty furlongs from them, the king caused his army to halt, and then drew it up in battle array. The peasants in the greatest terror came also and acquainted Darius with the arrival of the enemy, which he could not at first believe, imagining, as we have observed, that Alexander fled before him, and endeavoured to escape. This news threw his troops into the utmost confusion, who in that surprize ran to their arms with great precipitation and disorder.

The spot where the battle was fought lay near the city of Issus, which the mountains bounded on

one

one side, and the sea on the other. The plain that was situated between them both must have been considerably broad, as the two armies encamped in it; and that of Darius' was vastly numerous. The river Pinarius ran through the middle of this plain from the mountain to the sea, and divided it very near into two equal parts. The mountain formed a hollow like a gulph, the extremity of which in a curve line bounded part of the plain.

Alexander drew up his army in the following order. He posted at the extremity of the right wing, which stood near the mountains, the Argyraspides* commanded by Nicanor; then the Phalanx of Cœnus, and afterwards that of Perdiccas, which terminated in the centre of the main army. On the extremity of the left wing he posted the phalanx of Amyntas, then that of Ptolemy, and lastly, that of Meleager. Thus the famous Macedonian phalanx was formed, which we find was composed of six distinct corps or brigades. Each of these bodies was headed by able generals; but Alexander, being always generalissimo, had consequently the command of the whole army. The horse were placed on the two wings; the Macedonians, with the Thessalians, on the right, and those of Peloponnessus, with the other allies, on the left. Craterus commanded all the foot, which composed the left wing, and Parmenio the whole wing. Alexander had reserved to himself the command of the right. He had desired Parmenio to keep as near the sea as possible, to prevent the Barbarians from surrounding him; and Nicanor, on the contrary, was ordered to keep at some distance from the mountains

* *This was a body of infantry, distinguished by their silver shields, but much more so by their great bravery.*

mountains, to keep himself out of the reach of the arrows discharged by those who were posted there. He covered the horse of his right wing with the light horse of Protomachus and the Pœonians, and his foot with the bowmen of Antiochus. He reserved the Agrians (commanded by Attalus) who were greatly esteemed, and some forces that were newly arrived from Greece, to oppose those Darius had posted on the mountains.

As for Darius's army, it was drawn up in the following order. Having heard that Alexander was marching towards him in battle array, he commanded thirty thousand horse, and twenty thousand bowmen to cross the river Pinarius, that he might have an opportunity to draw up his army in a commodious manner on the hither side. In the centre he posted the thirty thousand Greeks in his service, who, doubtless, were the flower and chief strength of his army, and not at all inferior in bravery to the Macedonian phalanx, with thirty thousand Cardacians on their right, and as many on their left; the field of battle not being able to contain a greater number.

These were all heavily armed. The rest of the infantry, distinguished by their several nations, were ranged behind the first line. On the mountain which lay to their left, against Alexander's right wing, Darius posted twenty thousand men, who were so ranged (in several windings of the mountain) that some were behind Alexander's army, and others before it.

Darius, after having set his army in battle array, made his horse cross the river again, and dispatched the greatest part of them towards the sea against Parmenio, because they could fight on that spot with

the

the greatest advantage: the rest of his cavalry he sent to the left, towards the mountain. However, finding that these would be of no service on that side, because of the too great narrowness of the spot, he caused a great part of them to wheel about to the right. As for himself, he took his post in the centre of his army, pursuant to the custom of the Persian monarchs.

Alexander, observing that most of the enemy's horse was to oppose his left wing, which consisted only of those of Poloponessus, and some other allies, detached immediately to it the Thessalian cavalry, which he caused to wheel round behind his battalions, to prevent their being seen by the Barbarians. On the same side (to the left) he posted, before his foot, the Cretan bowmen, and the Thrasians of Sitalces (a king of Thrace) who were covered by the horse. The foreigners in his service were behind all the rest.

Perceiving that his right wing did not extend so far as the left of the Persians, which might surround and attack it in flank, he drew from the centre of his army two regiments of foot, which he detached thither, with orders for them to march behind to prevent their being seen by the enemy. He also reinforced that wing of his forces which he had opposed to the Barbarians on the mountains; for, seeing they did not come down, he made the Agrians and some other bowmen attack them, and drive them towards the summit of it; so that he left only three hundred horse to keep them in, and sent the rest, as I observed, to reinforce his right wing, which by this means extended farther than that of the Persians.

The

The two armies being thus drawn up in order of battle, Alexander marched very flowly, that his foldiers might take a little breath; fo that it was fuppofed they would not engage till very late: for Darius ftill continued with his army on the other fide of the river, in order not to lofe the advantageous fituation of his poft; and even caufed fuch parts of the fhore as were not craggy to be fecured with palifadoes, whence the Macedonians concluded that he was already afraid of being defeated, the two armies being come in fight. Alexander, riding along the ranks, called, by their feveral names, the principal officers both of the Macedonians and foreigners; exhorted the foldiers to fignalize themfelves, fpeaking to each nation according to its peculiar genius and difpofition. To the Macedonians he reprefented, " victories they had formerly gained in Europe; " the ftill recent glory of the battle of the Granicus; " the great number of cities and provinces they had " left behind them, all which they had fubdued." He added, that " by one fingle victory they would " poffefs themfelves of the Perfian empire; and that " the fpoils of the Eaft would be the reward of their " bravery and toils." The Greeks he animated, " by the remembrance of the many calamities which " the Perfians (thofe irreconcileable enemies to " Greece) had brought upon them;" and fet be- " fore them, the famous battle of Marathon, of " Thermopylæ, of Salamis, of Platææ, and the many " others by which they had required immortal glo- " ry." He bid the Illyrians and Thracians, nations who ufed to fubfift by plunder and rapine, " view " the enemies army, every part of which fhone with " gold and purple, and was not loaded fo much with
" arms

" arms as with booty. That they therefore should
" push forward (they who were men) and strip all
" those women of their ornaments; and exchange
" their mountains, covered perpetually with ice and
" snow, for the smiling plains and rich fields of
" Persia." The moment he had ended, the whole
army set up a shout, and eagerly desired to be led on
directly against the enemy.

Alexander had advanced at first very slowly, to
prevent the ranks, or the front of his phalanx, from
breaking, and halted by intervals: but when he was
got within bow-shot, he commanded all his right
(wing) to plunge impetuously into the river, purposely that they might surprise the Barbarians, come
sooner to a close engagement, and be less exposed to
the enemy's arrows; in all which he was very successful. Both sides fought with the utmost bravery and
resolution; and being now forced to fight close,
they charged on both sides sword in hand, when a
dreadful slaughter ensued; for they engaged man to
man, each aiming the point of his sword at the face
of his opponent. Alexander, who performed the
duty both of a private soldier and of a commander,
wished nothing so ardently as the glory of killing,
with his own hand, Darius, who being seated on a
high chariot, was conspicuous to the whole army;
and by that means was a powerful object, both to
encourage his own soldiers to defend, and the enemy
to attack him. And now the battle grew more furious and bloody than before; so that a great number
of Persian noblemen were killed. Each side fought
with incredible bravery. Oxatres, brother to Darius,
observing that Alexander was going to charge that
monarch with the utmost vigour, rushed before his

chariot

chariot with the horse under his command, distinguished himself above all the rest. The horses that drew Darius's chariot, being quite covered with wounds, began to prance about; and shook the yoke so violently, that they were upon the point of overturning the king, who, seeing himself going to fall alive into the hands of his enemies, leaped down, and mounted another chariot. The rest observing this, fled as fast as possible, and throwing down their arms, made the best of their way. Alexander had received a slight wound in his thigh, but happily it was not attended with ill consequences.

Whilst part of the Macedonian infantry (posted to the right) were carrying on the advantage they had gained against the Persians, the remainder of them who engaged the Greeks met with greater resistance. These observing that the body of infantry in question were no longer covered by the right (wing) of Alexander's army, which was pursuing the enemy, came and attacked it in flank. The engagement was very bloody, and victory a long time doubtful. The Greeks endeavoured to push the Macedonians into the river, and to recover the disorder into which the left wing had been thrown. The Macedonians also signalized themselves with the utmost bravery, in order to preserve the advantage which Alexander had just before gained, and support the honour of their phalanx, which had always been considered as invincible.

There was also a perpetual jealousy between these two nations (the Greeks and Macedonians) which greatly increased their courage, and made the resistance on each side very vigorous. On Alexander's side Ptolemy the son of Seleucus lost his life, with an hundred

dred and twenty more confiderable officers, who all had behaved with the utmoft gallantry.

In the mean time the right wing, which was victorious under its monarch, after defeating all who oppofed it, wheeled to the left againft thofe Greeks who were fighting with the reft of the Macedonian phalanx, whom they charged very vigoroufly; and attacking them in flank, entirely routed them.

At the very beginning of the engagement, the Perfian cavalry which was in the right wing (without waiting for their being attacked by the Macedonians) had croffed the river, and rufhed upon the Theffalian horfe, feveral of whofe fquadrons were broke by it. Upon this, the remainder of the latter, in order to avoid the impetuofity of the firft charge, and oblige the Perfians to break their ranks, made a feint of retiring, as terrified by the prodigious numbers of the enemy. The Perfians feeing this, were filled with boldnefs and confidence, and thereupon the greateft part of them advancing without order or precaution, as to a certain victory, had no thoughts but of purfuing the enemy. Upon this, the Theffalians feeing them in fuch confufion, faced about on a fudden, and renewed the fight with frefh ardour. The Perfians made a brave defence, till they faw Darius put to flight, and the Greeks cut to pieces by the phalanx.

The routing of the Perfian cavalry completed the defeat of the army. The Perfian horfe fuffered very much in the retreat, from the great weight of the arms of their riders; not to mention, that as they retired in diforder; and crowded in great numbers through paffes, they bruifed and unhorfed one another, and were more annoyed by their own foldiers than by by the enemy. Besides, the Thessalian cavalry pursued them with so much fury, that they were as much shattered as the infantry, and lost as many men.

With regard to Darius, as we before observed, the instant he saw his left wing broke, he was one of the first who fled in his chariot; but getting afterwards into craggy rugged places, he mounted on horseback, throwing down his bow, shield, and royal mantle. Alexander, however, did not attempt to pursue him, till he saw his phalanx had conquered the Greeks, and the Persian horse put flight; which was of great advantage to the prince that fled.

About eight thousand of the Greeks that were in Darius's service (with their officers at their head, who were very brave) retired over the mountains, towards Tripoli in Syria, where finding the transports which had brought them from Lesbos upon dry ground, they fitted out as many of them as suited their purpose, and burnt the rest, to prevent their being pursued.

As for the Barbarians, having exerted themselves with bravery enough in the first attack, they afterwards gave way in the most shameful manner; and, being intent upon nothing but saving themselves they took different ways. Some struck into the high road which led directly to Persia; others ran into woods and lonely mountains; and a small number returned to their camp, which the victorious enemy had already taken and plundered.

Sysigambis, Darius's mother, and that monarch's queen, who also was his sister, remained in it, with two of the king's daughters, a son of his (a child) and some Persian ladies. For the rest had been carried to Damascus, with part of Darius's treasure, and all,

such

such things as contributed only to the luxury and magnificence of his court. No more than three thousand talents were found in his camp; but the rest of the treasure fell afterwards into the hands of Parmenio, at his taking the city of Damascus.

Alexander, weary of pursuing Darius, seeing night draw on, and that it would be impossible for him to overtake that monarch, returned to the enemies camp, which his soldiers had just before plundered. Such was the end of this memorable battle, * fought the fourth year of Alexander's reign. The † Persians, either in the engagement or the rout, lost a great number of their forces, both horse and foot; but very few were killed on Alexander's side.

That very evening he invited the grandees of his court, and his chief officers, to a feast, at which he himself was present, notwithstanding the wound he had received, it having only grazed the skin. But they were no sooner set down at table, than they heard, from a neighbouring tent, a great noise intermixed with groans, which frighted all the company; insomuch that the soldiers, who were upon guard before the king's tent, run to their arms, being afraid of an insurrection. But it was found, that the persons who made this clamour were the mother and wife of Darius, and the rest of the captive ladies, who, supposing that prince dead, bewailed his loss, according to the custom of the Barbarians, with dreadful cries and howlings. An eunuch, who had seen Darius's cloak in the hands of a soldier, imagining he

---

* *A. M.* 367. *Ant. J. C.* 332.

† *According to Q. Curtius and Arian the Persians lost* 100,000 *foot and* 10,000 *horse. And the former historian relates, that no more than* 150 *horse and* 300 *foot, were lost on Alexander's side.*

he had killed him, and afterwards striped him of that garment, had carried them that false account.

We are told that Alexander, upon being told the reason of this false alarm, could not refrain from tears, when he considered the sad calamity of Darius, and the tender disposition of those princesses, whom his misfortunes only affected. He thereupon sent Leonatus, one of his chief courtiers, to assure them, that the man whose death they bewailed was alive. Leonatus, taking some soldiers with him, came to the tent of the princesses, and sent word, that he was come to pay them a visit in the king's name. The persons, who were at the entrance of the tent, seeing a band of armed men, imagined that their mistresses were undone ; and accordingly ran into the tent, crying aloud, that their last hour was come, and that soldiers were dispatched to murder them ; so that these princesses being seized with the utmost distraction, did not make the least answer, but waited in deep silence for the orders of the conqueror. At last, Leonatus having staid a long time, and seeing no one appear, left his soldiers at the door, and came into the tent : But their terror increased, when they saw a man enter among them without being introduced. They thereupon threw themselves at his feet, and intreated, that " before he put them to " death, they might be allowed to bury Darius after " the manner of their country ; and that when they " had paid this last duty to their king, they should " die contented." Leonatus answered, " That Da-" rius was living ; and that so far from giving them " any offence, they should be treated as queens, and " live in their former splendor." Sysigambis hearing this, began to recover her spirits, and permitted

Leonatus

Leonatus to give her his hand, to raife her from the ground. The next day Alexander, after vifiting the wounded, caufed the laſt honors to be paid to the dead, in prefence of the whole army, drawn up in the moſt fplendid order of battle. 'He treated the Perfians of diſtinction in the fame manner, and permitted Darius's mother to bury whatever perfons fhe pleafed, according to the cuſtom and ceremonies practifed in her country. However, this prudent princefs ufed that permiſſion in regard only to a few who were her near relations ; and that with fuch a modeſty and referve as fhe thought fuited her prefent condition. The king teſtified his joy and gratitude to the whole army, efpecially to the chief officers, whofe actions he applauded in the ſtrongeſt terms ; and he made prefents to all, according to their merit and ftation.

After Alexander had performed thefe feveral duties, truly worthy a great monarch, he fent a meffage to the queens, to inform them that he was coming to pay them a vifit ; and accordingly commanding all his train to withdraw, he entered the tent, accompanied only by Hephæſtion. He was his favourite, and as they had been brought up together, the king revealed his fecrets to him, and nobody elfe dared to fpeak fo freely to him, but even Hephæſtion made fo cautious and difcreet an ufe of that liberty, that he feemed to take it, not fo much out of inclination, as from a defire to obey the king, who would have it fo. They were of the fame age, but Hephæſtion was taller, fo that the queens took him at firſt for the king, and paid him their refpects as fuch : But fome captive eunuchs fhewing them Alexander, Syfigambis fell proſtrate before him, and begged his pardon ; declaring, that as fhe had never feen him, fhe hoped

that

that confideration would plead her apology. The king, raifed her from the ground, "Dear mother, (fays he) "you are not miftaken, for he alfo is an Alexander:" A fine expreffion which does honour to both! Had Alexander always thought and acted in this manner, he would juftly merited the title of Great; but fortune had not yet corrupted his foul. He bore her at firft with moderation and wifdom; but at laft fhe overpowered him, and he became unable to refift her.

Syfigambis, ftrongly affected with thefe teftimonies of goodnefs and humanity, could not forbear teftifying her gratitude upon that account. "Great prince
" (faid fhe) what words fhall I find to exprefs my
" thanks, in fuch a manner as may anfwer your gene-
" rofity! You call me your mother, and honour me
" ftill with the title of queen, whereas I confefs my-
" felf your captive. I know what I have been, and
" what I now am. I know the whole extent of my
" paft grandeur, and find I can fupport all the weight
" of my prefent ill fortune. But it will be glorious
" for you, as you now have an abfolute power over
" us, to make us feel it by your clemency only, and
" not by ill treatment."

The king after comforting the princeffes, took Darius' fon in his arms. This little child, without difcovering the leaft terror, embraced Alexander, who being affected with his confidence, and turning about to Hephæftion, faid to him; O that Darius had had fome portion of this tender difpofition.

To conclude, he treated thefe princeffes with fuch humanity, that nothing but the remembrance that they were captives, could have made them fenfible of their calamity, and of all the advantages they
poffeffed

possessed before, nothing was wanting with regard to Alexander, but that trust and confidence, which no one can repose in an enemy, how kindly soever he behaves.

SECT. VI. *Alexander marches victorious into Syria; the treasures deposited in Damascus are delivered to him. Darius writes a letter to Alexander in the most haughty terms, which he answers in the same stile. The gates of the city of Sidon are opened to him. Abdolonymus is placed upon the throne against his will. Alexander lays siege to Tyre, which at last, after having made a vigorous defence, is taken by storm. The fulfilling of the different prophecies relating to Tyre.*

(g) ALEXANDER set out towards Syria, after having consecrated three alters on the river Pinarius, the first to Jupiter, the second to Hercules, and the third to Minerva, as so many monuments of his victory. He had sent Parmenio to Damascus, in which Darius's treasure was deposited. The governor of the city, betraying his sovereign from whom he had now no further expectations, wrote to Alexander to acquaint him, that he was ready to deliver up into his hands, all the treasure and other rich stores of Darius. But being desirous of covering his treason with a specious pretext, he pretended that he was not secure in the city, so caused, by day-break, all the money and the richest things in it to be put on men's backs, and fled away with the whole, seemingly with intention to secure them, but in reality to deliver them

(g) *A. M.* 3672. *Ant. J. C.* 332.

them up to the enemy, as he had agreed with Parmenio, who had opened the letter addressed to the king. At the first sight of the forces which this general headed, those who carried the burthens being frighted, threw them down, and fled away, as did the soldiers who convoyed them, and the governor himself, who was most terrified. On this occasion immense riches were seen scattered up and down the fields; all the gold and silver designed to pay so great an army; the splendid equipages of so many great lords and ladies; the golden vases and bridles, magnificent tents, and carriages abandoned by their drivers; in a word, whatever the long prosperity and frugality of so many kings had amassed during many ages, was abandoned to the conqueror.

But the most moving part of this sad scene was to see the wives of the satraps and grandees of Persia, most of whom dragged their little children after them; so much the greater objects of compassion, as they were less sensible of their misfortune. Among these were three young princesses, daughters of Ochus, who had reigned before Darius; the widow of this Ochus; the daughter of Oxathres, brother to Darius; the wife of Artabazus, the greatest lord of the court, and his son Ilioneus. There also were taken prisoners the wife and son of Pharnabazus, whom the king had appointed admiral of all the coasts; three daughters of Mentor; the wife and son of Memnon, that illustrious general, insomuch that scarce one noble family in all Persia, but shared in this calamity.

There also was found in Damascus the ambassadors of the Grecian cities, particularly those of Lacedæmonia and Athens, whom Darius thought he had lodged in a safe asylum, when he put them under the protection of that traitor. Besides

Besides money and plate, which was afterwards coined, and amounted to immense sums, thirty thousand men, and seven thousand beasts laden with baggage, were taken. We find, by Parmenio's letter to Alexander, that he found in Damascus three hundred and twenty nine of Darius's concubines, all admirably well skilled in musick; and also a multitude of officers, whose business was to regulate and prepare every thing relating to entertainments, such as to make wreaths, to prepare perfumes and essences, to dress viands, to make pies, and all things in the pastry way, to preside over the wine cellars, to give out the wine, and such like. There were four hundred and ninety two of those officers; a train worthy a prince who runs to his destruction!

Darius, who a few hours before was at the head of so mighty and splendid an army, and who came into the field mounted on a chariot, with the pride of a conqueror, rather than with the equipage of a warrior, was flying over plains, which, from being before covered with the infinite multitude of his forces, now appeared like a desart or vast solitude. This ill-fated prince rode swiftly the whole night, accompanied by a very few attendants; for all had not taken the same road, and most of those who accompanied him could not keep up with him, as he often changed his horses. At last he arrived at *Sochus, where he assembled the remains of his army, which amounted only to four thousand men, including Persians as well as foreigners; and from hence he made all possible haste to Thapsacus, in order to have the Euphrates between him and Alexander.

In

* *This city was two or three days journey from the place where the battle was fought.*

In the mean time, Parmenio having carried all the booty into Damascus, the king commanded him to take care of it, and likewise of the captives. Most of the cities of Syria surrendered at the first approaches of the conquerer. Being arrived at Marathes, he received a letter from Darius, in which he stiled himself king, without bestowing that title on Alexander. He commanded, rather than intreated him, " to ask
" any money he should think proper, by way of ran-
" som for his mother, his wife, and children. That
" with regard to their dispute for empire, he might,
" if he thought proper, decide it in one general bat-
" tle, to which both parties should bring an equal
" number of troops : but that in case he were still
" capable of good counsel, he would advise him to
" rest contented with the kingdom of his ancestors,
" and not invade that of another : that they should
" henceforward live as good friends and faithful al-
" lies, that he himself was ready to swear to the ob-
" servance of these articles, and to receive Alexan-
" der's oath."

This letter, which breathed so unseasonable a pride and haughtiness, exceedingly offended Alexander. He therefore wrote the following answer :———
" Alexander the king to Darius. The ancient Da-
" rius whose name you assume, in former time en-
" tirely ruined the Greeks who inhabit the coasts of
" the Hellespont, and the Ionians, our ancient colo-
" nies. He next crossed the sea at the head of a
" powerful army, and carried the war into the very
" heart of Macedonia and Greece. After him,
" Xerxes made another descent with a dreadful
" number of Barbarians, in order to fight us ; and
" having been overcome in a naval engagement, he
" left,

" left, at his retiring, Mardonius in Greece, who
" plundered our cities, and laid waste our plains.
" But who has not heard that Philip, my father, was
" assassinated by wretches suborned thereto by your
" partizans, in hopes of a great reward? For it is
" customary with the Persians to undertake impious
" wars, and, when armed in the field, to set a price
" upon the heads of their enemies. And even you
" yourself, though at the head of a vast army, how-
" ever promised a thousand talents to any person
" who should kill me. I therefore only defend my-
" self, and consequently am not the aggressor. And
" indeed the Gods, who always declare for the just
" cause, have favoured my arms; and, aided by their
" protection, I have subjected a great part of Asia,
" and defeated you, Darius, in a pitched battle.
" However, though I ought not to grant any re-
" quest you make, since you have not acted fairly in
" this war; nevertheless, in case you will appear
" before me, in a supplicating posture, I give
" you my word, that I will restore to you, without
" any ransom, your mother, your wife, and children.
" I will let you see, that I know how to conquer, and
" to oblige the conquered. If you are afraid of sur-
" rendering yourself to me, I now assure you, upon
" my honour, that you may do it without the least
" danger. But remember, when you next write to
" me, that you write not only to a king, but to your
" king." Therfippus was ordered to carry this letter.

Alexander, marching from thence into Phœnicia,
the citizens of Byblos opened their gates to him.
Every one submitted as he advanced; but no people
did this with greater pleasure than the Sidonians.

The

The Persians had destroyed their city eighteen years before, and put all the inhabitants of it to the sword. Such of the citizens, who, upon account of their traffick, or for some other cause, had been absent, and by that means had escaped the general massacre, returned thither and rebuilt their city. But they had retained so violent a hatred of the Persians, that they were overjoyed at this opportunity to throw off their yoke; and indeed they were the first in that country who submitted to the king by their deputies, in opposition to Strato their king, who had declared in favour of Darius. Alexander dethroned him, and permitted Hephæstion to elect in his stead whomsoever of the Sidonians he should judge worthy of so exalted a station. Hephæstion was quartered at the house of two brothers, who were young, and of the most considerable family in the city; to these he offered the crown: but they refused it, telling him, that according to the laws of their country, no person could ascend the throne, unless they were of the blood royal. Hephæstion admiring this greatness of soul, which could contemn what others strive to obtain by fire and sword; " Continue (said he then) " in this way of thinking; you, who before were " sensible that it is much more glorious to refuse a " diadem, than to accept it. However, name " some person of the royal family, who may remem- " ber, when he is a king, that it was you who set the " crown upon his head." The brothers, observing that several through excessive ambition aspired to that high station, and to obtain it paid a very servile court to Alexander's favourites; declared that they did not know any person more worthy of the diadem than one Abdolonymus, descended though at a great distance,

tance, from the royal line; but who, at the same time, was so poor, that he was obliged to get his bread by day-labour in a garden without the city. His honesty and integrity had reduced him, as well as many more, to so extreme poverty. Solely intent upon his labour, he did not hear the clashing of arms which had shaken all Asia.

Immediately the two brothers went in search of Abdo'onymus with the royal garment, and found him weeding his garden. They then saluted him king, and one of them addressed him thus: " You must " now change your tatters for the dress I have brought " you. Put off the mean and contemptible habit " in which you have grown old; assume the senti- " ments of a prince; but when you are seated on " the throne, continue to preserve the virtue which " made you worthy of it. And when you shall have as- " cended it, and by that means become the supreme " dispenser of life and death over all your citizens, " be sure never to forget the condition in which, or " father for which, you was elected." Abdolony- mus looked upon the whole as a dream, and, unable to guess the meaning of it, asked if they were not ashamed to ridicule him in that manner. But, as he had less greater distance than suited their inclina- tion, they themselves washed him, and threw over his shoulders a purple robe, richly embroidered with gold. Then after repeated oaths of their being in earnest, they conducted him to the palace.

The news of this was immediately spread over the whole city. Most of the inhabitants were overjoyed at it, but some murmured, especially the rich, who, despising Abdolonymus's former abject state, could not forbear shewing their resentments upon this account

count in the king's court. Alexander commanded the new elected prince to be sent for; and after surveying him attentively a long time spoke thus: "Thy air and mein do not contradict what is related of thy extraction; but I should be glad to know with what frame of mind thou didst bear thy poverty."—"Would to the Gods (replied he) that I may bear this crown with equal patience. These hands have procured me all I desired; and whilst I possessed nothing, I wanted nothing." This answer gave Alexander an high idea of Abdolonymus' virtue; so that he presented him not only with all the rich furniture which had belonged to Strato, and part of the Persian plunder, but likewise annexed one of the neighbouring provinces to his dominions.

Syria and Phœnicia were already subdued by the Macedonians, the city of Tyre excepted. This city was justly entitled the queen of the sea, that element bringing to it the tribute of all nations. She boasted her having first invented navigation, and taught mankind the art of braving the wind and waves by the assistance of a frail bark. The happy situation of Tyre, the conveniency and extent of its ports, the character of its inhabitants, who were industrious, laborious, patient, and extremely courteous to strangers, invited thither merchants from all parts of the globe; so that it might be considered, not so much as a city belonging to any particular nation, as the common city of all nations, and the centre of commerce.

Upon Alexander's advancing towards it, the Tyrians sent him an embassy with presents for himself, and refreshments for his army. They were willing

to

to have him for their friend, but not for their master; so that when he discovered a desire of entering their city, in order to offer a sacrifice to Hercules, its tutelar god, they refused him admission. But this conqueror, after gaining so many victories, had too high an heart to put up such an affront, and thereupon was resolved to force them to it by a siege, which they, on the other side, were determined to sustain with the utmost vigour. The spring was now coming on. Tyre was at that time seated in an island of the sea, about a quarter of a league from the continent. It was surrounded with a strong wall an hundred and fifty feet high, which the waves of the sea washed; and the Carthagenians (a colony from Tyre) a mighty people, and sovereigns of the ocean, whose ambassadors were at that time in the city offering to Hercules, according to ancient custom, an annual sacrifice, had engaged themselves to succour the Tyrians. It was this made them so haughty. Firmly determined not to surrender, they fix machines on the ramparts, and on the towers, arm their young men, and build work-houses for the artificers, of whom there were great numbers in the city; so that every part resounded with the noise of warlike preparations. They likewise cast iron grapples, to throw on the enemy's works, and tear them away; as also cramp-irons, and such like instruments invented for the defence of the cities.

Alexander imagined that there were essential reasons why he should possess himself of Tyre. He was sensible that he could not invade Egypt easily, so long as the Persians should be masters of the sea; nor pursue Darius with safety, in case he should leave behind him so large an extent of country, the inhabitants

bitants of which were either enemies, or fufpected to be fo. He likewife was afraid, left fome infurrection fhould break out in Greece ; and that his enemies, after having retaken in his abfence the maritime cities of Afia-Minor, and increafed their fleet, would make his country the feat of war during his being employed in purfuing Darius in the plains of Babylon. Thefe apprehenfions were the more juftly grounded, as the Lacedæmonians had declared openly againft him ; and the Athenians fided with him more out of fear than affection. But, that in cafe he fhould conquer Tyre, all Phœnicia being then fubject to him, he would be able to difpofiefs the Perfians of half their naval army, which confifted of the fleet of that province ; and would foon make himfelf mafter of the ifland of Cyprus and of Egypt, which could not refift him the inftant he was become mafter at fea.

It was impoffible to come near this city in order to ftorm it, without making a bank which would reach from the continent to the ifland ; and an attempt of this kind would be attended with difficulties that were feemingly infurmountable. The little arm of the fea which feparated the ifland from the continent, was expofed to the weft wind, which often raifed fuch dreadful ftorms there, that the waves would in an inftant fweep away all works. Befides, as the city was furrounded on all fides by the fea, there was no fixing fcaling ladders, nor throwing up batteries, but at a diftance in the fhips ; and the wall, which projected into the fea toward the lower part, prevented people from landing ; not to mention that the military engines, which might have been put on board the gallies, could not do much execution, the waves were fo very tumultuous. But

But nothing was capable of checking or vanquishing the resolution of Alexander, who was determined to carry the city at any rate. However, as the few vessels he possessed lay at a great distance from him, and the siege of so strong a place might possibly last a long time, and so retard his other enterprises, he thought proper to endeavour an accommodation. Accordingly, he sent heralds, who proposed a peace between Alexander and their city; but these the Tyrians killed, contrary to the law of nations, and threw them from the top of the walls into the sea. Alexander exasperated at so cruel an outrage, formed a resolution at once, and employed his whole attention in raising a dike. He found in the ruins of old Tyre, which stood on the continent, and was called Palae-Tyros, materials to make piers, taking all the stones and rubbish from it. Mount Libanus, which was not far distant from it, so famous in scripture for its cedars, furnished him with wood for piles, and other timber-work.

The soldiers began the pier with great alacrity, being animated by the presence of their sovereign, who himself gave out all the orders; and who, knowing perfectly how to insinuate himself into, and gain the affections of his troops, excited some by praises, and others by slight reprimands, intermixed with kind expressions, and softened by promises. At first they advanced with pretty great speed, the piles being easily drove into the slime, which served as mortar for the stones; and as the place where these works were carrying on, was at some distance from the city, they went on without interruption. But the farther they went from the shore, the greater difficulties they met with; because the sea was deeper, and the workmen were very much annoyed by the darts difcharged from the top of the walls. The enemy who were mafters of the fea, coming forward in great boats, and razing every part of the dike, prevented the Macedonians from carrying it on with vigour. Then adding infults to their attacks, they cried aloud to Alexander's foldiers, " That it was a " noble fight to fee thofe conquerors, whofe names " were fo renowned all the world over, carrying " burthens on their backs like fo many beafts." And they would afterwards afk them in a contemptuous tone of voice, " whether Alexander was greater " than Neptune ; and if they pretended to prevail " over that God."

But thefe taunts did but inflame the courage of the foldiers. At laft the bank appeared above water, began to fhow a level of a confiderable breadth, and to approach the city. Then the befieged perceiving with terrour the vaftnefs of the work, which the fea had till then kept from their fight, came in their fhip-boats in order to view the bank, which was not yet very firm. Thefe boats were full of flingers, bowmen, and others who hurled javelins, and even fire ; and being fpread to the right and left about the bank, they fhot on all fides upon the workmen, feveral of whom were wounded ; it not being poffible for them to ward off the blows, becaufe of the great eafe and fwiftnefs with which the boats moved backwards and forwards ; fo that they were obliged to leave the work to defend themfelves. It was therefore refolved, that fkins and fails fhould be fpread to cover the workmen ; and that two wooden towers fhould be raifed at the head of the bank, to prevent the approaches of the enemy.

On

On the other side, the Tyrians made a descent on the shore, out of the view of the camp, where they landed some soldiers, who cut to pieces those that carried the stones; and on Mount Libanus there also were some Arabian peasants, who, meeting the Macedonians straggling up and down, killed near thirty of them, and took very near the same number. These small losses obliged Alexander to separate his troops into different bodies.

The besieged, in the mean time, employed every invention, every stratagem that could be found, to ruin the enemy's works. They took a transport vessel, and filling it with brushes, and such like dry materials, made a large enclosure near the prow, wherein they threw all these things, with sulphur and pitch, and other combustible matters. In the middle of this inclosure they set up two masts, to each of which they fixed two sailyards, on which were hung kettles full of oil, and such like unctuous substances. They afterwards loaded the hinder part of the vessel with stones and sand, in order to raise the prow; and taking advantage of a favourable wind, they towed it to sea by the assistance of their gallies. As soon as they were come near the towers they set fire to the vessel in question, and drew it towards the point or extremity of the bank. In the mean time the sailors, who were in it, leaped into the sea and swam away. Immediately the fire catched, with great violence, the towers, and the rest of the works which were at the head of the bank; and then the sail yards being drove backwards and forwards, threw oil upon the fire, which very much increased the flame. But, to prevent the Macedonians from extinguishing it, the Tyrians, who were in their gallies,

were

were perpetually hurling at the towers fiery darts and burning torches, infomuch that there was no approaching them. Several Macedonians loft their lives in a miferable manner on the bank; being either fhot through with arrows, or burnt to death; whilft others, throwing down their arms, leaped into the fea. But as they were fwimming away, the Tyrians, choofing to take them alive rather than kill them, maimed their hands with clubs and ftones; and after difabling them, carried them off. At the fame time the befieged, coming out of the city in little boats, beat down the edges of the bank, tore up its ftakes, and burnt the reft of the engines.

Alexander, though he faw moft of his defigns defeated, and his works demolifhed, was not at all dejected upon that account. His foldiers endeavoured, with redoubled vigour, to repair the ruins of the bank; and made and planted new machines with fo prodigious a fpeed, as quite aftonifhed the enemy. Alexander himfelf was prefent on all occafions, and fuperintended every part of the works. His prefence and great abilities advanced thefe ftill more, than the multitude of hands employed in them. The whole was near finifhed, and brought almoft to the wall of the city, when there arofe on a fudden an impetuous wind, which drove the waves with fo much fury againft the bank, that the cement and other things that bound it gave way, and the water rufhing through the ftones, broke it in the middle. As foon as the great heap of ftones which fupported the earth was thrown down, the whole funk at once, as into an abyfs.

Any warrior but Alexander would that inftant have quite laid afide his enterprife; and indeed he he himself debated whether he should not raise the siege. But a superiour power, who had foretold and sworn the ruin of Tyre, and whose orders this prince only executed, prompted him to continue the siege, and dispelling all his fear and anxiety, inspired him with courage and confidence, and fired the breasts of his whole army with the same sentiments. For now the soldiers, as if but that moment arrived before the city, forgetting all the toils they had undergone, began to raise a new mole, at which they worked incessantly.

Alexander was sensible, that it would not be possible for him either to complete the bank, or take the city, as long as the Tyrians should continue masters at sea. He therefore resolved to assemble before Sidon his few remaining gallies. At the same time, the kings of Aradus and Byblos, hearing that Alexander had conquered their cities, abandoned the Persian fleet, joined him with theirs, and that of the Sidonians, which made in all eighty sail. There arrived also much about the same time, ten gallies from Rhodes, three from Solæ, and Mallos, ten from Lycia, and one from Macedonia of fifty oars. A little after, the kings of Cyprus, hearing that the Persian army had been defeated near the city of Issus, and that Alexander had possessed himself of Phœnicia, brought him a reinforcement of upwards of one hundred and twenty gallies.

The king, whilst his soldiers were preparing the ships and engines, took some troops of horse, with his own regiment of guards, and marched towards a mountain of Arabia, called Antilibanus. The tender regard he had for an old gentleman, formerly his tutor, who was absolutely resolved to follow his pupil,

pil, exposed Alexander to very great danger. This was Lysimachus, who gave the name of Achilles to his scholar, and called himself Phœnix. When the king was got to the foot of the mountain, he leaped from his horse, and began to walk. His troops got a considerable way before him, it was already late, and Alexander not being willing to leave his preceptor, who was very corpulent, and scarce able to walk, he by that means was separated from his little army, accompanied only by very few soldiers; and in this manner spent the whole night very near the enemy, who were so numerous, that they might easily have overpowered him. However, his usual good fortune and courage extricated him from this danger; so that, coming up afterwards with his forces, he advanced forward into the country, took all the strong places either by force or capitulation, and returned the eleventh day to Sidon, where he found Alexander, son of Polemocrates, who had brought him a reinforcement of four thousand Greeks from Peloponessus.

The fleet being ready, Alexander took some soldiers from among his guards, and these he embarked with him, in order to employ them in close fight with the enemy; and then set sail towards Tyre, in battle array. He himself was at the point or extremity of the right wing, which extended itself towards the main ocean, being accompanied by the kings of Cyprus and Phœnicia; the left was commanded by Craterus. The Tyrians were at first determined to give battle; but after they heard of the uniting of these forces, and saw the army advance, which made a great appearance (for Alexander had halted to wait the coming up of his left wing)

they

they kept all their gallies in the harbours, to prevent the enemy from entering them. When the king saw this, he advanced nearer the city; and finding it would be impossible for him to force the port which lay towards Sidon, because of the great narrowness of the entrance, and its being defended by a large number of gallies, all whose prows were turned towards the main ocean, he only funk three of them which lay without, and afterwards came to an anchor with his whole fleet, pretty near the bank, along the shore, where his ships rode in safety.

Whilst all these things were doing, the new bank was carried on with great vigour. The workmen threw into the sea whole trees with all their branches on them; and laid great stones over these, on which they put other trees, and the latter they covered with clay, which served instead of mortar. Afterwards heaping more trees and stones on these, the whole thus joined together, formed one intire body. This bank was made wider than the former ones, in order that the towers that were built in the middle might be out of the reach of such arrows as should be shot from those ships which might attempt to break down the edge of the bank. The besieged, on the other side, exerted themselves with extraordinary bravery, and did all that lay in their power to stop the progress of the work. But nothing was of so much service to them as their divers, who swimming under water, came unperceived quite up to the bank, and with hooks drew such branches to them as projected beyond the work; and pulling forward with great strength, forced away every thing that was over them: However, after many delays, the patience of the workmen surmounting every obstacle, it was at last

last finished in its utmost perfection. The Macedonians placed military engines of all kinds on the bank, in order to shake the walls with battering rams, and hurl on the besieged arrows, stones, and burning torches.

At the same time Alexander ordered the Cyprian fleet, commanded by Andromachus, to take its station before the harbour which lay towards Sidon; and that of Phœnicia before the harbour on the other side of the bank facing Egypt; towards that part where his own tent was pitched; and enabled himself to attack the city on every side. The Tyrians, in their turn, prepared for a vigorous defence. On that side which lay towards the bank, they had erected towers on the wall, which was of a prodigious height, and of a proportionable breadth, the whole built with great stones cemented together with mortar. The access to any part was very near as difficult, the enemy having fenced the foot of the wall with great stones, to keep the Greeks from approaching it. The business then was, first to draw these away, which could not be done but with the utmost difficulty, because, as the soldiers stood in ships, they could not keep very firm on their legs. Besides, the Tyrians advanced with covered gallies, and cut the cables which held the ships at anchor; so that Alexander was obliged to cover in like manner, several vessels of thirty rowers each, and to station these cross-wise, to secure the anchors from the attacks of the Tyrian gallies. But still divers came and cut them unperceived, so that they were at last forced to fix them with iron chains. After this, they drew these stones with cable ropes, and carrying them off with engines, they were thrown to the bottom of the

the sea, where it was not possible for them to do any further mischief. The foot of the wall being thus cleared, the vessels had very easy access to it. In this manner the Tyrians were invested on al sides, and attacked at the same time both by sea and land.

The Macedonians had joined (two and two) gallies with four men chained to each oar, in such a manner, that the prows were fastened, and the sterns so far distant one from the other, as was necessary for the pieces of timber between them to be of a proper length. After this they threw from one stern to the other sail-yards, which were fastened together by planks laid crofs-wife, in order for the soldiers to stand fast on the space. The gallies being thus equipped, they rowed towards the city, and shot (under covert) against those who defended the walls, the prows serving them as so many parapets. The king caused them to advance about midnight, in order to surround the walls, and make a general assault. The Tyrians now gave themselves for lost, when on a sudden the sky was overspread with such thick clouds, as quite took away the faint glimmerings of light which before darted through the gloom. The sea rises by insensible degrees; and the billows being swelled by the fury of the winds, rife to a dreadful storm. The vessels dash one against the other with so much violence, that the cables, which before fastened them together, are either loosened, or break to pieces; the planks split, and, making a horrible crash, carry off the soldiers with them; for the tempest was so furious, that it was not possible to manage or steer gallies thus fastened together. The soldier was a hindrance to the sailor, and the sailor to the soldier; and, as happens on such occasions, these

obeyed

whose business it was to command; fear and anxiety throwing all things into confusion. But now the rowers exerted themselves with so much vigour, that they got the better of the sea, and seemed to tear their ships out of the waves. At last they brought them near the shore, but the greatest part in a shattered condition.

At the same time there arrived at Tyre, thirty ambassadors from Carthage, who did not bring the least succours, though they had promised such mighty things. Instead of this, they only made excuses, declaring that it was with the greatest grief the Carthagenians found themselves absolutely unable to assist the Tyrians in any manner, for that they themselves were engaged in a war, not as before for empire, but to save their country. And indeed the Syracusans were laying waste all Africa at that time, with a powerful army, and had pitched their camp not far from the walls of Carthage. The Tyrians, though frustrated in this manner of the great hopes they had conceived, were no ways dejected. They only took the wise precautions to send most of their women and children to Carthage, in order that they might be in a condition to defend themselves to the last extremity, and bear more courageously the greatest calamities which might befall them, when they had once lodged, in a secure asylum, what they most valued in the world.

There was in the city a brazen statue of Apollo, of an enormous size. This colossus had formerly stood in the city of Gela and Sicily, the Carthegenians having taken it about the year 412 before Christ, had given it by way of present, to the city of Tyre, which they always considered as the mother of Carthage.

The

The Tyrians had set it up in their city, and worship was paid to it. During the siege, on a dream which one of the citizens had, the Tyrians imagined that Apollo was determined to leave them, and go over to Alexander. Immediately they fastened with a gold chain his statue to Hercules's altar, to prevent the deity in question from leaving them. For these people were silly enough to believe, that after his statue was thus fastened down, it would not be possible for him to make his escape; and that he would be prevented from doing so by Hercules, the tutelar god of the city.

Some of the Tyrians proposed the restoring of a sacrifice which had been discontinued for many ages; and this was, to sacrifice a child born of free parents, to Saturn. The Carthagenians, who had borrowed this sacrilegious custom from their founders, preserved it till the destruction of their city; and had not the old men, who were invested with the greatest authority in Tyre, opposed this cruelly-superstitious custom, a child would have been butchered on this occasion.

The Tyrians, finding their city exposed every moment to be taken by storm, resolved to fall upon the Cyprian fleet, which lay at anchor off Sidon. They took the opportunity to do this at a time when the seamen of Alexander's fleet were dispersed up and down; and that he himself was withdrawn to his tent, pitched on the sea-shore. Accordingly, they came out, about noon, with thirteen gallies, all manned with choice soldiers who were used to sea-fights; and rowing with all their might, came thundering on the enemy's vessels. Part of them they found empty, and the rest had been manned in great haste.

haste. Some of these they sunk, and drove several of them against the shores, where they dashed to pieces. The loss would have been still greater, had not Alexander, the instant he heard of this sally, advanced at the head of his whole fleet with all imaginable dispatch against the Tyrians. However, these did not wait their coming up, but withdrew into the harbour, after having also lost some of their ships.

And now the engines playing, the city was warmly attacked on all sides, and as vigorously defended. The besieged, taught and animated by imminent danger, and the extreme necessity to which they were reduced, invented daily new arts to defend themselves, and repulse the enemy. They warded off all the darts discharged from the balisters against them by the assistance of turning wheels, which either broke them to pieces, or carried them another way. They deadened the violence of the stones that were hurled at them, by setting up a kind of sails and curtains made of a soft substance, which easily gave way. To annoy the ships which advanced against their walls, they fixed grapling-irons and scythes to joists or beams; then straining their catapultas (an enormous kind of cross-bows) they laid those great pieces of timber upon them instead of arrows, and and shot them off on a sudden at the enemy. These crushed some to pieces, by their great weight; and the hooks or pensile scythes with which they were armed, tore others to pieces, and did considerable damage to their ships. They also had brazen shields, which they drew red-hot out of the fire; and, filling these with burning sand, hurled them in an instant from the top of the wall upon the enemy. There was nothing the Macedonians so much dreaded as

this

this laft invention, for, the moment this burning fand got to the flefh, through the crevices in the armour, it pierced to the very bone, and ftuck fo clofe, that there was no pulling it off; fo that the foldiers throwing down their arms, and tearing their clothes to pieces, were in this manner expofed, naked and defencelefs, to the fhot of the enemy.

It was then Alexander, difcouraged at fo vigorous a defence, debated ferioufly, whether it would not be proper for him to raife the fiege, and go for Egypt: for, after having over run Afia with prodigious rapidity, he found his progrefs unhappily retarded; and loft, before a fingle city, the opportunity of executing a great many projects of infinitely greater importance. On the other fide, he confidered that it would be a great blemifh to his reputation, which had done him greater fervice than his arms, fhould he leave Tyre behind him, and thereby prove to the world, that he was not invincible. He therefore refolved to make a laft effort with a great number of fhips, which he manned with the flower of his army. Accordingly, a fecond naval engagement was fought, in which the Tyrians, after fighting with intrepidity, were obliged to draw off their whole fleet towards the city. The king purfued their rear very clofe, but was not able to enter the harbour, being repulfed by arrows fhot from the walls: However, he either took or funk a great number of their fhips.

Alexander, after letting his forces repofe themfelves two days, advanced his fleet and his engines, in order to attempt a general affault. Both the attack and defence were now more vigorous than ever. The courage of the combatants increafed with the

danger:

danger; and each side, animated by the most powerful motives, fought like lions. Wherever the battering-rams had beat down any part of the wall, and the bridges were thrown out, instantly the Argyraspides mounted the breach with the utmost valour, being headed by Admetus, one of the bravest officers in the army, who was killed by the thrust of a * Partisan, as he was encouraging his soldiers. The presence of the king, and especially the example he set, fired his troops with unusual bravery. He himself ascended one of the towers, which was of a prodigious height, and there was exposed to the greatest danger his courage had ever made him hazard; for, being immediately known by his insignia and the richness of his armour, he served as a mark for all the arrows of the enemy. On this occasion he performed wonders; killing, with javelins, several of those who defended the wall; then advancing nearer to them, he forced some with his sword, and others with his shield, either into the city or the sea; the tower where he fought almost touching the wall. He soon went over it, by assistance of floating bridges, and followed by the nobility, possessed himself of two towers, and the space between them. The battering-rams had already made several breaches; the fleet had forced into the harbour; and some of the Macedonians had possessed themselves of the towers which were abandoned. The Tyrians, seeing the enemy masters of their ramparts, retired towards an open place, called Agenor, and there stood their ground; but Alexander marching up with his regiment of body-guards, killed part of them and obliged the rest

---

* *A kind of halbert.*

reſt to fly. At the ſame time, Tyre being taken on that ſide which lay towards the harbour, the Macedonians ran up and down every part of the city, ſparing no perſon who came in their way, being highly exaſperated at the long reſiſtance of the beſieged, and the barbarities they had exerciſed towards ſome of their comrades who had been taken in their return to Sidon, and thrown from the battlements, after their throats had been cut in the ſight of the whole army.

The Tyrians, ſeeing themſelves overpowered on on all ſides, ſome fly to the temples, to implore the aſſiſtance of the gods; others, ſhutting themſelves in their houſes, eſcape the ſword of the conqueror, by a voluntary death, in fine, others ruſh upon the enemy, firmly reſolved to ſell their lives at the deareſt rate. Moſt of the citizens were got on the houſetops, whence they threw ſtones, and whatever came to firſt to hand, upon ſuch as advanced forward the city. The king gave orders for killing all the inhabitants (thoſe excepted who had ſheltered themſelves in the temples) and to ſet fire to every part of Tyre. Although this order was publiſhed by ſound of trumpet, yet not one perſon who carried arms ſlew to the aſylums. The temples were filled with ſuch old men and children only as had remained in the city. The old men waited at the doors of their houſes, in expectation every inſtant of being ſacrificed to the rage of the ſoldiers. It is true, indeed, that the Sidonian ſoldiers, who were in Alexander's camp, ſaved great numbers of them. For, having entered the city indiſcriminately with the conquerors, and calling to mind their ancient affinity with the Tyrians (Agenor having founded both Tyre and
Sidon)

Sidon) they, for that reason, carried off great numbers privately on board their ships, and conveyed them to Sidon. By this kind deceit, fifteen thousand were saved from the rage of the conqueror; and we may judge of the greatness of the slaughter, from the number of soldiers who were cut to pieces on the rampart of the city only, who amounted to six thousand. However, the king's anger not being fully appeased, he exhibited a scene, which appeared dreadful even to the conquerors; for two thousand men remaining after the soldiers had been glutted with slaughter, Alexander caused them to be fixed upon crosses along the sea shore. He pardoned the ambassadors of Carthage, who were come to their metropolis to offer up a sacrifice to Hercules, according to annual custom. The number of prisoners, both foreigners and citizens, amounted to thirty thousand, who were all sold. As for the Macedonians, their loss was very inconsiderable. Alexander himself sacrificed to Hercules, and conducted the ceremony with all his land forces under arms, in concert with the fleet. With regard to the statue of Apollo, before mentioned he took off the chains from it, restored it to its former liberty, and commanded that this *god should thenceforwards be surnamed Philalexander, that is, the friend of Alexander. The city of Tyre was taken about the end of September, after having sustained seven months siege.

Thus were accomplished the menaces which God had pronounced by the mouth of his prophets against the city of Tyre. Nebuchadnezzar had begun to execute those threats, by besieging and taking it; and they were completed by the sad catastrophe we have here described.

(i) Tyre

(i) Tyre was built by the Sidonians, two hundred and forty years before the building of the temple of Jerusalem; for this reason it is called by Isaiah, The daughter of Sidon. It soon surpassed its mother city in extent, power and riches.

(k) It was besieged by Salmanasar, and alone resisted the united fleets of the Assyrians and Phœnicians; a circumstance which greatly heightened its pride.

(l) Nebuchadnezzar laid siege to Tyre at the same time that Ithobalus was king of that city; but did not take it till thirteen years after. But before it was conquered, the inhabitants had retired, with most of their effects, into a neighbouring island, where they built a new city. The old one was razed to the very foundation, and has since been no more than a village, known by the name of Palœ-Tyrus, or ancient Tyre: but the new one rose to greater power than ever.

It was in this great and flourishing condition, when Alexander besieged and took it. And here begins the seventy years obscurity and oblivion, in which it was to lie, according to Isaiah. It was indeed soon repaired, because the Sidonians, who entered the city with Alexander's army, saved fifteen thousand of their citizens, who, after their return, applied themselves to traffick, and repaired the ruins of their country with incredible application; besides which, the women and children, who had been sent to Carthage, and lodged in a place of safety, returned to it at the same time. But Tyre was confined

---

(i) A. M 2992.   Ant. J. C.   1712.
(k) A. M 3285   Ant. J. C.   719.
(l) A. M. 342.   Ant. J. C.   572.

fined to the island in which it stood. Its trade extended no farther than the neighbouring cities, and it had lost the empire of the sea. And when, eighteen years after, Antigonus besieged it with a strong fleet, we do not find that the Tyrians had any maritime forces to oppose him. This second siege, which reduced it a second time to captivity, plunged it into the state of oblivion from which it endeavoured to extricate itself; and this oblivion continued the exact time foretold by Isaiah.

(m) Tyre, before the captivity of the Jews in Babylon, was considered as one of the most ancient and flourishing cities of the world. Its industry and very advantageous situation had raised it to the sovereignty of the seas, and made it the centre of all the trade in the universe; all nations contributed to the increase of its riches, splendour, and power.

And Tyre, on the other side, dispersed this varied abundance over all kingdoms, and infected them with its corrupt manners, by inspiring mankind with a love for ease, vanity, luxury, and voluptuousness.

(n) A long, uninterrupted series of prosperities had swelled the pride of Tyre. She delighted to consider herself as the queen of cities; whose correspondents are illustrious princes, whose rich traders dispute for superiority with kings: who sees every maritime power, either as her allies or dependents; and who made herself necessary or formidable to all nations.

Tyre had now filled up the measure of her iniquity, by her impiety against God, and her barbarity exercised against his people. She had rejoiced over the

ruins

(m) Ezek. xxvi. *and* xxvii. *throughout. Ezek* xxvii. 4, 25.
(n) Ezek. xxvi. 17. xxviii. 3, 4, 25—32, 33.

ruins of Jerusalem, in the insulting words following. *(o)* "Behold then the gates of this so populous city are broken down. Her inhabitants shall come to me, and I will enrich myself with her spoils, now she is laid waste." *(p)* She was not satisfied with having reduced the Jews to a state of captivity, notwithstanding the alliance between them; with selling them to the Gentiles, and delivering them up to their most cruel enemies: *(q)* She likewise had seized upon the inheritance of the Lord, and carried away from his temple the most precious things, to enrich therewith the temples of her Idols.

(r) This profanation and cruelty drew down the vengeance of God upon Tyre. God is resolved to destroy her, because she relied so much upon her own strength, her wisdom, and her alliances. He therefore brought against her Nebuchadnezzer, that king of kings, to overflow her with his mighty host, as with waters that overspread their banks, in order to demolish her ramparts, to ruin her proud palaces, to deliver up her merchandizes and treasures to the soldier, and to raze Tyre to the very foundation, after having set fire to it, and either extirpated or dispersed all its inhabitants.

But Tyre, after she had recovered her losses, and repaired her ruins, forgot her former state of humiliation; *(s)* she still was puffed up with the glory of possessing the empire of the sea; of being the seat of universal commerce; of giving birth to the most famous colonies, of having within her walls merchants,

(o) Ezek. xxvii. 2.
(p) Joel iii. 2. 8.
(q) Joel iii. 2. 4. 7. Amos i. 9. 10.
(r) Jerem. xlvii. 2. 6. Ezek. xxvii. 3. 12. and 19. xxvii. 27. 34.
(s) Isai. xxiii. 3, 4, 7, 8, 12.

chants, whose credit, riches, and splendour, equalled them to the princes and great men of the earth.

(t) But since this city, corrupted by pride, by avarice and luxury, has not profited by the first lesson which God had given her, in the person of the king of Babylon; and that, after being opprest by all the forces of the east, she still would not learn to confide no longer in the false and imaginary supports of her own greatness: (u) God foretells her another chastisement, which he will send upon her from the west, near four hundred years after the first, (v) her destruction will come from thither, that is, Macedonia; from a kingdom so weak and obscure, that it had been despised a few years before; a kingdom whence she could never have expected such a blow. Tyre, possessed with an opinion of her own wisdom, and proud of her fleets, of her immense riches, which she heaped up as mire in the streets, and also protected by the whole power of the Persian empire, does not imagine she has any thing to fear from those new enemies, who being situated at a great distance from her, without either money, strength or reputation; having neither harbours nor ships, and being quite unskilled in navigation; cannot therefore, as she imagines, annoy her with her land forces. (w) Tyre looks upon herself as impregnable, because she is defended by lofty fortifications, and surrounded on all sides by the sea, as with a mote and girdle: nevertheless, Alexander, by filling up the arm of the sea which separates her from the continent, will force off her girdle, and demolish
those

(t) Ezek. xxviii. 2.
(u) Isa. xxiii. 13.
(v) 1 Maccab. 1. 1.   Zech. ix. 2. 5.
(w) Isa. xxiii. 10   1. 13.

those ramparts which served her as a second enclosure.

Tyre, thus dispossessed of her dignity as queen and as a free city, boasting no more her diadem nor her girdle, will be reduced during seventy years, to the mean condition of a slave. (*x*) The Lord hath purposed it, to stain the pride of all glory, and to bring into contempt all the honourable of the earth. (*y*) Her fall will drag after it the ruin of trade in general, and she will prove to all cities a subject of sorrow and groans, by making them lose the present means and the future hopes of enriching themselves.

SECT. VII. *Darius writes a second letter to Alexander. Journey of the latter to Jerusalem. The honour he pays to Jaddus the high-priest. He is shewn those prophecies of Daniel which relate to himself. The king grants great privileges to the Jews, but refuses them to the Samaritans. He besieges and takes Gaza, enters Egypt, and subdues that country. He there lays the foundation of Alexandria, then goes into Lybia, where he visits the temple of Jupiter Ammon, and causes himself to be declared the son of that god. His return into Egypt.*

WHILST Alexander was carrying on the siege of Tyre, he had received a second letter from Darius, who at last gave him the title of king. "He offered " him ten thousand talents as a ransom for the cap- " tive princesses, and his daughter Statira in marri- " age,

(*x*) *Isa*. xxiii. 9.
(*y*) *Isa*. xxii. 1. 11. 14.

" age, with all the country he had conquered as far
" as the Euphrates, Darius hinted to him the incon-
" stancy of fortune; and described, in the most
" pompous terms the numberless troops who were
" still under his command. Could he (Alexander)
" think, that it was so very easy to cross the Eu-
" phrates, the Tygris, the Araxes, and the Hydaf-
" pes, which were as so many bulwarks to the Per-
" sian empire? That he should not always be shut
" up between rocks and passes: that they ought
" both to appear in a plain, and that then Alexander
" would be ashamed to come before him with only
" a handful of men." The king hereupon summoned a council, in which Parmenio was of opinion,
that he ought to accept of those offers, declaring he
himself would agree to them were he Alexander.
And so would I, replied Alexander, were I Parmenio.
He therefore returned the following answer: " That
" he did not want the money Darius offered him:
" that it did not become Darius to offer a thing he
" no longer possessed, or pretend to distribute what he
" had entirely lost, that in case he was the only per-
" son who did not know which of them was
" superior, a battle would soon determine it. That
" he should not think to intimidate with rivers, a
" man who had crossed so many seas. That to
" whatsoever place he might find it proper to retire,
" Alexander would not fail to find him out." Darius, upon receiving this answer, lost all hopes of an
accommodation, and prepared again for war.

From Tyre, Alexander marched to Jerusalem,
firmly resolved to shew it no more favour than he
had done the former city; and for this reason. The
Tyrians were so much employed in traffick, that they
quite

quite neglected hufbandry, and brought moft of their corn and other provifions from the conutries in their neighbourhood : Galilea, Samaria, and Judea furnifhed them with the greateft quantities. At the fame time that Alexander laid fiege to their city, he himfelf was obliged to fend for provifions from thofe countries : he therefore fent commiffaries to fummon the inhabitants to fubmit, and furnifh his army with whatever they might want. The Jews, however, defired to be excufed, alledging, that they had taken an oath of fidelity to D rius; and perfifted in anfwering, that they would never acknowledge any other fovereign as long as he was living. The Samaritans, however, did not imitate them in this particular; for they fubmitted with chearfulnefs to Alexander, and even fent him eight thoufand men, to ferve at the fiege of Tyre, and in other places.

Alexander, being little ufed to fuch an anfwer as he received from the Jews, refolved the inftant he had conquered Tyre, to march againft the Jews, and pun'fh their difobedience as rigoroufly as he had done that of the Tyrians.

In this imminent danger, Jaddus, the high-prieft, who governed under the Perfians, feeing himfelf expofed with all the inhabitants, to the wrath of the conqueror, had recourfe to the protection of the Almighty, gave orders for the offering up publick prayers to implore his affiftance, and made facrifices. The night after, God appeared to him in a dream, and bid him, " To caufe flowers to be fcattered up
" and down the city; to fet open all the gates, and
" and go cloathed in in his pontifical robes, with all
" the priefts dreffed alfo in their veftments, and all
" the reft cloathed in white, to meet Alexander, and
" not

"not to fear any evil from that king, inasmuch as he would protect them." This command was punctually obeyed; and accordingly this august procession, the very day after, marched out of the city to an eminence called Saphia* whence there was a view of all the plain, as well as of the temple and city of Jerusalem. Here the whole procession waited the arrival of Alexander.

The Syrians and Phœnicians, who were in his army, were persuaded that the wrath of this prince was so great, that he would certainly punish the high-priest after an exemplary manner, and destroy that city in the same manner as he had done Tyre; and flushed with joy upon that account, they waited in expectation of glutting their eyes with the calamities of a people to whom they bore a mortal hatred. As soon as the Jews heard of the king's approach, they set out to meet him with all the pomp before described. Alexander was struck at the sight of the high-priest, in whose mitre and forehead a golden plate was fixed, on which the name of God was written. The moment the king perceived the high-priest, he advanced towards him with an air of the most profound respect; bowed his body, adored the august name upon his front, and saluted him who wore it with a religious veneration. Then the Jews surrounding Alexander, raised their voices to wish him every kind of prosperity. All the spectators were seized with inexpressible surprize; they could scarce believe their eyes; and did not know how to account for a sight so contrary to their expectation, and so vastly improbable.

Parmenio,

---

* *The Hebrew word* Saphia, *signifies to discover from far, as from a tower or centry box.*

Parmenio, who could not yet recover from his astonishment, asked the king how it came to pass that he, who was adored by every one, adored the high-priest of the Jews. "I do not (replied Alex-
"ander) adore the high-priest, but God whose mi-
"nister he is; for whilst I was at Dia, in Macedo-
"nia (my mind wholly fixed on the great design of
"the Persian war) as I was revolving the methods
"how to conquer Asia, this very man, dressed in
"the same robes, appeared to me in a dream; ex-
"horted me to banish every fear, bid me cross the
"the Hellespont boldly; and assured me that God
"would march at the head of my army, and give
"me the victory over that of the Persians."
Alexander added, that the instant he saw this priest, he knew him by his habit, his stature, his hair, and his face, to be the same person whom he had seen at Dia; that he was firmly persuaded, it was by the command, and under the immediate conduct of heaven, that he had undertaken this war; that he was sure he should overcome Darius hereafter, and destroy the empire of the Persians; and that this was the reason why he adored this God in the person of his priest. Alexander, after having thus answered Parmenio, embraced the high-priest, and all his brethren; then walking in the midst of them, he arrived at Jerusalem, where he offered sacrifices to God, in the temple, after the manner prescribed to him by the high-priest.

The high-priest, afterwards, shewed him those passages in the prophecies of Daniel * which are

K spoken

---

* *The reader may find those prophecies in Dan.* 11. 20. 21. 37. *Ibid. ver.* 35. *Dan.* iv. 32. 34. 35. 36. *Dan.* vii. 2. 3 4. 5. 6. *Dan.* xi. 2. *Dan.* viii.

spoken of that monarch. We may eafily figure to ourfelves the great joy and admiration with wh'ch Alexander was filled, upon hearing fuch clear, fuch circumftantial, and advantageous promifes. Before he left Jerufalem, he affembled the Jews, and bid them afk any favour whatfoever. They anfwered, that their requeft was, to be allowed to live according to the laws which their anceftors had left them, and to be exempt the feventh year, from their ufual tribute; and for this reafon, becaufe they were forbid, by their laws, to fow their fields, and confequently could have no harveft. Alexander granted their requeft, and, upon the high-prieft's befeeching him to fuffer the Jews, who lived in Babylonia and Media, to live likewife agreeable to their own laws, he alfo indulged them in this particular, with the umoft humanity; and faid further, that in cafe any of them would be willing to ferve under his ftandards, he would give them leave to follow their own way of worfhip, and to obferve their refpective cuftoms: Upon which offer, great numbers lifted themfelves.

He was fcarce come from Jerufalem, but the Samaritans waited upon him with great pomp and ceremony, humbly intreating him to do them alfo the honour to vifit their temple. As thefe had fubmitted voluntarily to Alexander, and fent him fuccours, they imagined that they deferved his favour much more than the Jews; and flattered themfelves that they fhould obtain the fame, and even much greater indulgence. It was in this view they made the pompous proceffion above mentioned, in order to invite Alexander to their city; and the eight thoufand men they had fent to ferve under him,

joined

joined in the requeft made by their countrymen. Alexander thanked them courteoufly; but faid, that he was obliged to march into Egypt, and therefore had no time to lofe; however, that he would vifit their city at his return, in cafe he had opportunity. They then befought him to exempt them from paying a tribute every feventh year; upon which Alexander afked them, whether they were Jews? They made an ambiguous anfwer, which the king not having time to examine, he alfo fufpended this matter till his return, and immediately continued his march towards Gaza.

Upon his arrival before that city, he found it provided with a ftrong garrifon, commanded by Betis, one of Darius's eunuchs. This governor, who was a brave man, and very faithful to his fovereign, defended it with great vigour againft Alexander. As this was the only inlet or pafs into Egypt, it was abfolutely neceffary for him to conquer it, and therefore he was obliged to befiege it. But although every art of war was employed, notwithftanding his foldiers fought with the utmoft intrepidity, he was however forced to lie two months before it. Exafperated at its holding out fo long, and his receiving two wounds, he was refolved to treat the governor, the inhabitants, and foldiers, with a barbarity abfolutely inexcufable; for he cut ten thoufand men to pieces, and fold all the reft, with their wives and children, for flaves. When Betis, who had been taken prifoner in the laft affault, was brought before him, Alexander, inftead of ufing him kindly, as his valour and fidelity juftly merited, this young monarch, who otherwife efteemed bravery even in an enemy, fired on that occafion with an infolent joy,

fpoke

spoke thus to him: Betis, thou shalt not die the death thou defiredft. Prepare therefore to fuffer all thofe torments which revenge can invent. Betis, looking upon the king not only with a firm, but an haughty air, did not make the leaft reply to his menaces; upon which the king, more enraged than before at his difdainful filence—" Obferve, faid he, I " befeech you, that dumb arrogance: Has he bended " the knee? Has he fpoke but even fo much as one "" fubmiffive word? But I will conquer this obftinate " filence, and will force groans from him, if I can. " draw nothing elfe." At laft Alexander's anger rofe to fury; his conduct now beginning to change with his fortune: Upon which he ordered a hole to be made through his heels, when a rope being put thro" them, and this being tied to a chariot, he ordered his foldiers to drag Betis round the city till he died. He boafted his having imitated on this occafion, Achilles, from whom he was defcended; who, as Homer relates, caufed the dead body of Hector to be dragged in the fame manner, round the walls of Troy.

He fent the greateft part of the plunder he found in Gaza to Olympias, to Cleopatra his fifter, and to his friends. He alfo prefented Leonidas, his preceptor, with five hundred quintals (or a hundred weight) of frankincenfe, and an hundred quintals of myrrh; calling to mind a caution Leonidas had given him when but a child, and which feemed, even at that time, to prefage the conqueft this monarch had lately atchieved. For Leonidas, obferving Alexander take up whole handfuls of incenfe at a facrifice, and throw it into the fire, faid to him: Alexander, when you fhall have conquered the country which produces thefe fpices, you then may be as profufe of

incenfe

incense as you please; but till that day comes, be sparing of what you have. The monarch therefore writ to Leonidas as follows: I send you a large quantity of incense and myrrh, in order that you may no longer be so reserved and sparing in your sacrifices to the Gods.

As soon as Alexander had ended the siege of Gaza, he left a garrison there, and turned the whole power of his arms towards Egypt. In seven days march he arrived before Pelusium, whither a great number of Egyptians had assembled with all imaginable diligence to recognise him for their sovereign.

The hatred these people bore to the Persians was so great, that they valued very little who should be their king, provided they could but meet with a hero to rescue them from the insolence and indignity with which themselves, and those who professed their religion, were treated. For, how false soever a religion may be (and it is scarce possible to imagine one more absurd than that of the Egyptians) so long as it continues to be the established religion, the people will not suffer it to be insulted, nothing affecting their minds so strongly, nor firing them to a greater degree. Ochus, who had caused their god Apis to be murthered, in a manner highly injurious to themselves and their religion; and the Persians, to whom he had left the government, continued to make the same mock of that deity. Thus several circumstances had rendered the Persians so odious, that, upon Amyntas's coming a little before with a handful of men, he found them prepared to join, and assist him in expelling the Persians.

This Amyntas had deserted from Alexander, and entered into the service of Darius. He had commanded

manded the Grecian forces at the battle of Issus; and having fled into Syria, by the country lying towards Tripoli, with four thousand men, he had there seized upon as many vessels as he wanted, burned the rest, and immediately set sail towards the island of Cyprus, and afterwards towards Pelusium, which he took by surprise, upon feigning that he had been honoured with a commission from Darius, appointing him governor of Egypt, in the room of Sabaces, killed in the battle of Issus. As soon as he found himself possessed of this important city, he threw off the mask, and made public pretensions to the crown of Egypt; declaring, that the motive of his coming was to expel the Persians. Upon this a multitude of Egyptians, who wished for nothing so earnestly as to free themselves from these insupportable tyrants, went over to him. He then marched directly for Memphis, the capital of the kingdom; when, coming to a battle, he defeated the Persians, and shut them up in the city. But, after he had gained this victory, having neglected to keep his soldiers together, they straggled up and down in search of plunder; which the enemy seeing, they sallied out upon such as remained, and cut them to pieces, with Amyntas their leader.

This event, so far from lessening the aversion the Egyptians had for the Persians, increased it still more; so that the moment Alexander appeared upon the frontiers, the people, who were all disposed to receive that monarch, ran in crouds to submit to him. His arrival, at the head of a powerful army, presented them with a secure protection, which Amyntas could not afford them; and, from this consideration, they all declared openly in his favour. Mazœus, who

who commanded in Memphis, finding it would be to no purpose for him to resist so triumphant an army, and that Darius, his sovereign, was not in a condition to succour him; he therefore set open the gates of the city to the conqueror, and gave up eight hundred talents, about one hundred and forty thousand pounds, and all the king's furniture. Thus Alexander possessed himself of all Egypt, without meeting with the least opposition.

At Memphis he formed a design of visiting the temple of Jupiter Ammon. This temple was situated in the midst of the sandy desarts of Lybia, and twelve days journey from Memphis. Ham, the son of Noah, first peopled Egypt and Lybia, after the flood; and when idolatry began to gain ground in the world some time after, he was the chief deity of those two countries in which his descendants had continued. A temple was built to his honour in the midst of these desarts, upon a spot of pretty good ground, about two leagues broad, which formed a kind of island in a sea of sand. It is he whom the Greeks call Jupiter, and the Egyptians Ammon. In process of time these two names were joined, and he was called Jupiter-Ammon.

The motive of this journey, which was equally rash and dangerous, was owing to a ridiculous vanity. Alexander, having read in Homer, and other fabulous authors of antiquity, that most of their heroes were represented as sons of some deity; and as he himself was desirous of passing for an hero, he was determined to have some god for his father. Accordingly, he fixed upon Jupiter Ammon for this purpose, and began by bribing the priests, and teaching them the part they were to act.

(b) Alexander

(*b*) Alexander therefore sets out; and going down from the river Memphis, till he came to the sea, he coasts it; and after having passed Canopus, he observes, opposite to the island of Pharos, a spot he thought very well situated for the building of a city. He himself drew the plan of it, and marked out the several places where the temples and public squares were to be erected. For the building it, he employed Dinocrates the architect, who had acquired great reputation by his rebuilding, at Ephesus, the temple of Diana, which Herostratus had burnt. This city he called after his own name, and it afterwards rose to be the capital of the kingdom. As its harbour, which was very commodious, had the Mediterranean on one side, and the Nile and red-sea in its neighbourhood, it drew all the traffic of the east and west; and thereby became, in a very little time, one of the most flourishing cities in the universe.

Alexander had a journey to go of sixteen hundred stadia, or fourscore French leagues, to the temple of Jupiter Ammon; and most of the way was through sandy desarts. The soldiers were patient enough for the two first days march, before they arrived in the vast dreadful solitudes; but as soon as they found themselves in vast plains, covered with sands of a prodigious depth, they were greatly terrified. Surrounded, as with a sea, they gazed round as far as their sight could extend, to discover, if possible, some place that was inhabited; but all in vain, for they could not perceive so much as a single tree, nor the least footsteps of any land that had been cultivated. To increase their calamity, the water, that they had brought in goat-skins, upon camels, now failed; and

there

(*b*) *A. M.* 3673. *Ant. J. C.* 331.

there was not so much as a single drop in all that sandy desart. They therefore were reduced to the sad condition of dying almost with thirst; and not to mention the danger they were in of being buried under mountains of sand, that are sometimes raised by the winds; and which had formerly destroyed fifty thousand of Cambyses's troops. Every thing was by this time scorched to so violent a degree, and the air become so hot, that the men could scarcely breathe; when on a sudden, whether by chance, say the historians, or the immediate indulgence of heaven, the sky was so completely overspread with thick clouds, that they hid the sun, which was a great relief to the army; though they were still in prodigious want of water. But the storm having discharged itself in a violent rain, every soldier got as much as he wanted; and some had so violent a thirst, that they stood with their mouths open, and catched the rain as it fell.

They were several days in crossing these desarts, and, upon their arriving near the place where the oracle stood, they perceived a great number of ravens flying before the most advanced standard. These ravens, sometimes, flew to the ground when the army marched slowly; and, at other times, advanced forward, to serve them as guides, till they, at last, came to the temple of the god. A vastly surprising circumstance is, that although this oracle be situated in the midst of an almost boundless solitude, it nevertheless is surrounded with a grove, so very shady, that the sun-beams can scarcely pierce it; not to mention that this grove or wood is watered with several springs of fresh water, which preserve it in perpetual verdure. It is related, that near this

K 3. grove

grove there is another, in the midst of which is a fountain, called the water, or fountain of the sun. At day-break it is luke warm, at noon cold; but in the evening it grows warmer infensibly, and at midnight is boiling hot; after this, as day approaches, it decreases in heat, and continues this viciffitude for ever.

The god who is worshiped in this temple, is not represented under the form which painters and sculptors generally give to gods; for he is made of emeralds, and other precious stones, and from the head to the * navel, resembles a ram. The king being come into the temple, the senior priest declared him to be the son of Jupiter; and affured, that the god himself bestowed this name upon him. Alexander accepted it with joy, and acknowledged Jupiter as his father. He afterwards asked the priest, whether his father Jupiter had not allotted him the empire of the whole world? to which the priest, who was as much a flatterer as the king was vainglorious, answered, that he should be monarch of the universe. At last, he inquired, whether all his father's murderers had been punished; but the priest replied, that he blasphemed; that his father was immortal; but that with regard to the murderers of Philip, they had all been extirpated; adding, that he should be invincible, and afterwards take his feat among the deities. Having ended his sacrifice, he offered magnificent presents to the god, and did not forget the priests, who had been so faithful to his interest.

Swelled with the spendid title of the son of Jupiter,

---

* *This paſſage in Quintus Curtius is pretty difficult, and is variously explained by interpreters.*

er, and fancying himself raised above the human species, he returned from his journey as from a triumph. From that time, in all his letters, his orders and decrees, he always wrote in the style following: ALEXANDER KING, SON OF JUPITER AMMON: In answer to which, Olympias, his mother, one day made a very witty remonstrance in a few words, by desiring him not to quarrel any longer with Juno.

Whilst Alexander prided himself in these chimeras, and tasted the great pleasure in vanity made him conceive from this pompous title, every one derided him in secret; and some, who had not yet put on the yoke of abject flattery, ventured to reproach him upon that account; but they paid very dear for that liberty, as the sequel will show.

Alexander, upon his return from the temple of Jupiter Ammon, being arrived at the Palus Mareotis, which was not far from the island of Pharos, made a visit to the new city, part of which was new built.

He took the best method possible to people it, inviting thither all sorts of persons, to whom he offered the most advantageous conditions. He drew to it, among others, a considerable number of Jews, by allowing them very great privileges; for, he not only left them the free exercise of their religion and laws, but put them on the same foot in every respect with the Macedonians, whom he settled there. From thence he went to Memphis, where he spent the winter.

Varro observes, that at the time this king built Alexandria, the use of Papyrus (for writing) was found in Egypt; but this I shall mention elsewhere.

During Alexander's stay in Memphis, he settled

the

the affairs of Egypt, suffering none but Macedonians to command the troops. He divided the country into districts, over each of which he appointed a lieutenant, who received orders from himself only; not thinking it safe to entrust the general command of all the troops to one single person, in so large and populous a country. With regard to the civil government, he invested one Doloaspes with the whole power of it; for being desirous that Egypt should still be governed by its ancient laws and customs, he was of opinion that a native of Egypt, to whom they must be familiar, was fitter for that office than any foreigner whatsoever.

To hasten the building of this new city, he appointed Cleomenes inspector over it; with orders for him to levy the tribute which Arabia was to pay. But this Cleomenes was a very wicked wretch, who abused his authority, and oppressed the people with the utmost barbarity.

(c) SECT. VIII. *Alexander, after his return from Egypt, resolves to go in pursuit of Darius, at his setting out he hears of the death of that monarch's queen. He causes the several honours to be paid her which were due to her rank. He passes the Euphrates and Tygris, and comes up with Darius. The famous battle of Arbela.*

ALEXANDER having settled the affairs of Egypt, set out from thence about spring-time, to march into the east against Darius. In his way through Palestine

(c) *A. M.* 3674. *Ant. J. C.* 330.

tine, he heard news which gave him great uneasiness. At his going into Egypt, he had appointed Andromachus, whom he highly esteemed, governor of Syria and Palestine. Andromachus coming to Samaria to settle some affairs in that country, the Samaritans mutinied; and setting fire to the house in which he was, burnt him alive. Alexander was highly exasperated against them for this cruel action, and put to death all those who had any hand in it, banished the rest from the city of Samaria, supplying their room with a colony of Macedonians, and divided the rest of their lands among the Jews.

He made some stay in Tyre, to settle the various affairs of the countries he left behind him, and advanced towards new conquests.

He was scarce set out, but an Eunuch brought word that Darius's consort was dead in child-bed. Hearing this, he returned back, and went into the the tent of Sysigambis, whom he found bathed in tears, and lying on the ground, in the midst of the young princesses, who also were weeping. Alexander consoled them in so kind and tender a manner, as plainly shewed that he himself was deeply and sincerely afflicted. He caused her funeral obsequies to be performed with the utmost splendour and magnificence.

Immediately after those solemnities were over, Alexander set out upon his march, and arrived with his whole army at Thapsachus, where he passed a bridge that lay across the Euphrates, and continued his journey towards the Tygris, where he expected to come up with the enemy. Darius had already made overtures of peace to him twice, but finding at last that there was no hopes of their succeeding,

L

unless he signed the whole empire to him, he therefore prepared himself again for battle. For this purpose, he assembled in Babylon an army half as numerous again as that of Issus, and marched it towards Nineveh; his forces covered all the plains of Mesopotamia. Advice being brought, that the enemy was not far off, he caused Satropates, colonel of the cavalry, to advance at the head of a thousand chosen horse; and likewise gave six thousand to Mazæ, governor of the province; all of whom were to prevent Alexander from crossing the river, and to lay waste the country through which that monarch was to pass; but he arrived too late.

Of all the rivers of the east this is the most rapid; and not only a great number of rivulets mix in its waves, but those also drag along great stones, so that it is named Tygris, by reason of its prodigious rapidity, an arrow being so called in the Persian tongue. Alexander sounded those parts of the river which were fordable, and there the water, at the entrance, came up to the horses bellies. Having drawn up his infantry in the form of a half moon, and posted his cavalry on the two wings, they advanced to the current of the water with no great difficulty, carrying their arms over their head. The king walked on foot among the infantry, and was the first who appeared on the opposite shore, where he pointed out with his hand the ford to the soldiers. But it was with the greatest difficulty they kept themselves above water; because of the impetuosity of the stream. At last, they all passed over that part of the ford where the water was shallowest, and the stream less impetuous; but with the loss however of the greatest part of their baggage.

The

The king having encamped two days near the river, commanded his soldiers to be ready for marching on the morrow; but about nine or ten in the evening, the moon, first lost its light, and appeared afterwards quite sullied, and, as it were tinctured with blood. Now as this happened just before a great battle was going to be fought, the doubtful success of which, filled the army with sufficient disquietude, they were first struck with a religious awe, and, being afterwards seized with fear, they cried out, "That heaven displayed the marks of its anger; "and that they were dragged against the will of it, "to the extremities of the earth; that rivers oppo- "sed their passage; that the stars refused to lend "their light; and that they could now see nothing "but deserts and solitude; that merely to satisfy "the ambition of one man, so many thousands shed "their blood; and that for a man who contemned "his own country, disowned his father, and pretend- "ed to pass for a god."

These murmurs were rising to an open insurrection, when Alexander whom nothing could intimidate, summoned the officers of his army into his tent, and commanded such of the Egyptian soothsayers as were best skilled in the knowledge of the stars to declare what they thought of this phænomenon. These knew very well the natural causes of eclipses of the moon; but, without entering into physical enquiries, they contented themselves with saying, that the sun was on the side of the Greeks, and the moon on that of the Persians; and that whenever it suffered an eclipse, it always threatened the latter with some grievous calamity, whereof they mentioned several examples, all which

they

they gave as true and indisputable. Superstition has a surprising ascendant over the minds of the vulgar. How headstrong and inconsistent soever they may be, yet if they are once struck with a vain image of religion, they will sooner obey soothsayers than their leaders. The answer made by the Egyptians being dispersed among the soldiers, it revived their hopes and courage.

The king, purposely to take advantage of this ardour, began his march after midnight. On his right hand lay the river Tygris, and on his left the mountains called Gordyæi. At day-break the scouts whom he had sent to view the enemy, brought word that Darius was marching towards him; upon which he immediately drew up his forces in battle-array, and set himself at their head. However, it was afterwards found, that they were only a detachment of a thousand horse that were going upon discoveries, and which soon retired to the main army. Nevertheless, news was brought the king, that Darius was now but an hundred and fifty * stadia from the place where they were.

Not long before this, some letters had been intercepted, by which Darius solicited the Grecian soldiers either to kill or betray Alexander. Nothing can reflect so great an odium on the memory of this prince, as an attempt of that kind; an attempt so abject and black, and more than once repeated. Alexander was in doubt with himself, whether it would be proper for him to read these letters in a full assembly, relying as much on the affection and fidelity of the Greeks, as on that of the Macedonians.

But

* *Seven or eight leagues.*

But Parmenio diffuaded him from it; declaring that it would be dangerous even to awake such thoughts in the minds of soldiers; that one only was sufficient to strike the blow; and that avarice was capable of attempting the most enormous crimes. The king followed this prudent counsel, and ordered his army to march forward.

Although Darius had twice sued in vain for peace, and imagined that he had nothing to trust to but to his arms; nevertheless, being overcome by the advantageous circumstances which had been told him concerning Alexander's tenderness and humanity towards his family, he dispatched ten of his chief relations, who were to offer him fresh conditions of peace more advantageous than the former; and to thank him for the kind treatment he had given his family. Darius had, in the former proposals, given him up all the provinces as far as the river Halys; but now he added the several territories situated between the Hellespont and the Euphrates, that is, all he already possessed. Alexander made the following answer: " Tell your sovereign, that thanks, between
" persons who make war against each other, are superfluous; and that, in case I behaved with clemency towards his family, it was for my own sake, and not for his; in consequence of my own inclination, and not to please him. To insult the unhappy is a thing to me unknown. I do not attack either prisoners or women, and turn my rage against such only as are armed for the fight. Did Darius sue for peace in a sincere view, I then would debate on what is to be done; but since he still continues by letters and by money, to spirit up
" my

" my soldiers to betray me, and my friends to mur-
" der me, I therefore am determined to pursue him
" with the utmost vigour; and that not as enemy,
" but a poisoner, and an assassin. It, indeed be-
" comes him, to offer to yield up to me what I am
" possessed of! Would he be satisfied with ranking
" himself as a second to me, without pretending to
" be my equal, I might possibly then hear him.
" Tell him that the world will not permit two suns,
" nor two sovereigns. Let him therefore choose either
" to surrender to-day, or to fight me to-morrow, and
" not flatter himself with the hopes of obtaining bet-
" ter success than he has hitherto had."

The ambassadors having leave to depart, returned back and told Darius that he must prepare for battle. The latter pitched his camp near a village Gaugemala, and the river Bumela, in a plain at a considerable distance from Arbela. He had before levelled the spot which he pitched upon for the field of battle, in order that his chariots and cavalry might have full room to move in; recollecting, that his fighting in the straits of Cilicia had lost him the battle fought there. At the same time, he had prepared * crows' feet to annoy the enemy's horse.

Alexander, upon hearing this news, continued four days in the place he then was, to rest his army, and surrounded his camp with trenches and palisades; for he was determined to leave all his baggage, and the useless soldiers in it, and march the remainder against the enemy, with no other equipage than the arms they carried. Accordingly, he set out about nine

---

* *Crows' feet is an instrument composed of iron spikes Several of these are laid in fields through which the cavalry are to march, in order that they may run into the horses feet.*

nine in the evening, in order to fight Darius at daybreak; who, upon this advice, had drawn up his army in order of battle. Alexander alfo marched in battle-array; for both armies were within two or three leagues of each other. When he was arrived at the mountains, where he could difcover the enemy's whole army, he halted; and, having affembled his general officers, as well Macedonians as foreigners, he debated whether they fhould engage immediately, or pitch their camp in that place. The latter opinion being followed, becaufe it was judged proper for them to view the field of battle, and the manner in which the enemy was drawn up, the army encamped in the fame order in which he had marched; during which Alexander, at the head of his infantry, lightly armed, and his royal regiments, marched round the plain in which that battle was to be fought.

Being returned, he affembled his general officers a fecond time, and told them, that there was no occafion for his making a fpeech, becaufe their courage and great actions were alone fufficient to excite them to glory; that he defired them only to reprefent to the foldiers, that they were not to fight, on this occafion, for Phoenicia or Egypt, but for all Afia, which would be poffeffed by him who fhould conquer; and that, after having gone through fo many provinces; and left behind them fo great a number of rivers and mountains, they could fecure their retreat no otherwife than by gaining a complete victory. After this fpeech, he ordered them to take fome repofe.

It is faid, that Parmenio advifed him to attack the enemy in the night-time, alledging that they might eafily easily be defeated, if fallen upon by surprise, and in the dark; but the king answered so loud, that all present might hear him, that it did not become Alexander to steal a victory, and therefore he was resolved to fight and conquer in broad day-light. Darius, fearing he should be attacked at unawares, because he had not entrenched himself, obliged his soldiers to continue the whole night under arms, which proved of the highest prejudice to him in the engagement.

Alexander, who in the crisis of affairs used always to consult soothsayers, observing, very exactly, whatever they enjoined, in order to obtain the favour of the gods, finding himself upon the point of fighting a battle, the success of which was to give empire to the conqueror, sent for Aristander, in whom he reposed the greatest confidence. He then shut himself up with the soothsayer, to make some secret sacrifices; and afterwards offered up victims to Fear, which he doubtless did to prevent his army from being seized with dread, at the sight of the formidable army of Darius. The soothsayer, dressed in his vestments, holding vervain, with his head veiled, first repeated the prayers which the king was to address to Jupiter, to Minerva, and to Victory. The whole being ended, Alexander went to bed, to repose himself the remaining part of the night. As he revolved in his mind, not without some emotion, the consequence of the battle, which was upon the point of being fought, he could not sleep immediately. But his body being oppressed, in a manner; by the anxiety of his mind, he slept soundly the whole night, contrary to his usual custom: so that when his generals were assembled at day-break before his tent, to receive

ceive his orders, they were greatly surprised to find that he was not awake; upon which, they themselves commanded the soldiers to take some refreshment. Parmenio having at last awaked him, and seeming surprised to find him in so calm and sweet a sleep, just as he was going to fight a battle, in which his whole fortune lay at stake: How could it be possible, said Alexander, for us not to be calm, since the enemy is coming to deliver himself into our hands? Immediately he took up his arms, mounted his horse, and rode up and down the ranks, exhorting the troops to behave gallantly, and, if possible, to surpass their ancient fame, and the glory they had hitherto acquired. Soldiers, on the day of battle, imagine they see the fate of the engagement painted in the face of their general. As for Alexander, he had never appeared so calm, so gay, nor so resolute. The serenity and security which they observed in him, were in a manner so many assurances of the victory.

There was a great difference between the two armies with respect to numbers, but much more so with regard to courage. That of Darius consisted at least* of six hundred thousand foot, and forty thousand horse; and the other of no more than forty thousand foot, and seven or eight thousand horse: But the latter was all fire and strength; whereas, on the side of the Persians, it was a prodigious assemblage of men, not of soldiers; an empty phantom rather than a real army.

Both sides were disposed in very near the same array. The forces were drawn up in two lines, the cavalry

* *According to several historians it amounted to upwards of a million of men.*

cavalry on the two wings, and the infantry in the middle; the one and the other being under the particular conduct of the chiefs of each of the different nations that compofed them; and commanded in general, by the principle crown-officers. The front of the battle (under Darius) was covered with two hundred chariots, armed with fcythes, and with fifteen elephants, the king taking his poft in the centre of the firft line. Befides the guards, which were the flower of his forces, he alfo had fortified himfelf with the Grecian infantry, whom he had drawn up near his perfon; believing this body only capable of oppofing the Macedonian phalanx, as his army fpread over a much greater fpace of ground than that of the enemy, he intended to furround, and to charge them, at one and the fame time, both in front and flank.

But Alexander had guarded againft this, by giving orders to the commanders of the fecond line, that in cafe they fhould be charged behind, to face about to that fide; or elfe to draw up their troops in form of a gibbet, and to cover the wings, in cafe the enemy fhould charge them in flank. He had pofted, in the front of his firft line, the greateft part of his bowmen, flingers, hurlers of javelins, in order that thefe might make head againft the chariots armed with fcythes; and frighten the horfes, by difcharging at them a fhower of arrows, javelins, and ftones. Thofe who led on the wings, were ordered to extend them as wide as poffible; but in fuch a manner as. not to weaken the main body. As for the baggage and the captives, among whom were Darius's mother and children, they were left in the camp, under a fmall guard. Parmenio commanded, as he had always done, the left wing, and Alexander the right.

When

When the two armies came in view, Alexander, who had been shown the several places where the chariots were hid, extended more and more towards the right to avoid them; and the Persians advanced forward in proportion. Darius, being afraid left the Macedonians should draw him from the spot of ground he had levelled, and carry him into another that was rough and uneven, commanded the cavalry in his left wing, which spread much farther than that of the enemy's right, to march right forward, and wheel about upon the Macedonians in flank, to prevent them from extending their troops further. Then Alexander difpatched against them the body of horse in his service commanded by Menidas, but, as these were not able to make head against the enemy, because of their prodigious numbers, he reinforced the... with the Pæoneans, whom Aretas commanded, and with the foreign cavalry. * Besides the advantage of numbers, they had that also of their coats of mail, which secured themselves, and their horses much more. Alexander's cavalry was prodigiously annoyed: However, they marched to the charge with great bravery, and at last put them to flight.

Upon this, the Persians opposed the chariots armed with scythes against the Macedonian Phalanx, in order to break it, but with little success. The noise which the soldiers, who were lightly armed, made, by striking their swords against their bucklers, and the arrows which flew on all sides, frighted the horses, and made a great number of them turn back against their own troops. Others, laying hold of the

horses

---

* *Some relate that the Barbarians gave way at first, but soon returned to the charge.*

horses bridles, pulled the riders down, and cut them to pieces. Part of the chariots drove between the battalions, which opened to make way for them, as they had been ordered to do, by which means they did little or no execution.

Alexander, seeing Darius set his whole army in motion in order to charge him, employed a stratagem to encourage his soldiers. When the battle was at the hottest, and the Macedonians were in the greatest danger, Aristander, the soothsayer, cloathed in his white robes, holding a branch of laurel in his hand, advances among the combatants as he had been instructed by the king; and, crying that he saw an eagle hovering over Alexander's head (a sure omen of victory) he showed with his finger the pretended bird to the soldiers; who, relying upon the sincerity of the soothsayer, fancied they also saw it; and thereupon renewed the attack with greater chearfulness and ardour than ever. Then the king perceiving that Aretas (after having charged the cavalry, and put them into disorder, upon their advancing to surround his right wing) had begun to break the foremost ranks of the main body of the Barbarian army; he marched after Aretas, with the flower of his troops, when he quite broke the enemy's left wing, which had already begun to give way; and without pursuing the forces which he had thrown into disorder, he wheeled to the left, in order to fall upon the body in which Darius had posted himself. The presence of the two kings inspired both sides with vigour. Darius was mounted on a chariot, and Alexander on horseback; both surrounded with their bravest officers and soldiers, whose only endeavour was to save the lives of their respective princes,

at

at the hazard of their own. The battle was obstinate and bloody. Alexander, having wounded Darius's equerry with a javelin, the Persians, as well as the Macedonians, imagined that the king was killed; upon which the former, breaking aloud into the most dismal sounds, the whole army was seized with the greatest consternation. The relations of Darius, who were at his left hand, fled away with the guards, and so abandoned the chariot; but those who were on his right, took him into the centre of their body. Historians relate, that this prince having drawn his scimitar, reflected whether he ought not to lay violent hands upon himself, rather than fly in an ignominious manner: But perceiving from his chariot that his soldiers still fought, he was ashamed to forsake them; and, as he was divided between hope and despair, the Persians retired insensibly, and thinned their ranks; when it could no longer be called a battle, but a slaughter. Then Darius, turning about his chariot, fled with the rest; and the conqueror was now wholly employed in pursuing him.

Whilst all this was doing in the right wing of the Macedonians, where the victory was not doubtful; the left wing, commanded by Parmenio, was in great danger. A detachment of the Persian, Indian and Parthian horse, which were the best in all the Persian army, having broke through the infantry on the left, advanced to the very baggage. The moment the captives saw them arrive in the camp, they armed themselves with every thing that came first to hand, and, reinforcing their cavalry, rushed upon the Macedonians who were now charged both before and behind. They, at the same time, told Sysigambis,

M that

that Darius had won the battle (for this they believed); that the whole baggage was plundered, and that she was now going to recover her liberty. But this princess, who was a woman of great wisdom, though this news affected her in the strongest manner, could not easily give credit to it; and being unwilling to exasperate, by too hasty a joy, a conqueror, who had treated her with so much humanity, she did not discover the least emotion; did not once change countenance, nor let drop a single word; but in her usual posture, calmly waited till the event should denounce her fate. --

Parmenio, upon the first report of this attack, had dispatched a messenger to Alexander, to acquaint him with the danger to which the camp was exposed, and to receive his orders. " Above all things (said " the prince) let him not weaken his main body; " let him not mind the baggage, but apply himself " wholly to the engagement; for victory will " not only restore us our own possessions, but also " give those of the enemy into our hands." The general officers, who commanded the infantry which formed the centre of the second line, seeing the enemy were going to make themselves masters of the camp and baggage made a half-turn to the right, in obedience to the orders which had been given, and fell upon the Persians behind, many of whom were cut to pieces, and the rest obliged to retire; but as these were horse, the Macedonian foot could not follow them.

Soon after, Parmenio himself was exposed to much greater peril. Mazæus, having rushed upon him with all his cavalry, charged the Macedonians in flank, and began to surround them. Immediately Parmenio sent

Alexander advice of the danger he was in; declaring, that in cafe he were not immediately fuccoured, it would be impoffible for him to keep his foldiers together. The prince was actually purfuing Darius, and, fancying he was almoft come up with him, rode with the utmoft fpeed. He flattered himfelf, that he fhould abfolutely put an end to the war, in cafe he fhould but feize his perfon. But, upon this news, he turned about, in order to fuccour his left wing; fhuddering with rage to fee his prey and victory torn in this manner from him; and complaining againft fortune, for having favoured Darius more in his flight, than himfelf in the purfuit of that monarch.

Alexander, in his march, met the enemy's horfe who had plundered the baggage; all which were returning in good order, and retiring back, not as foldiers who had been defeated, but almoft as if they had gained the victory. And now the battle became more obftinate than before; for, the Barbarians marching clofe in columns, not in order of battle but that of a march, it was very difficult to break through them; and they did not amufe themfelves with throwing javelins, nor with wheeling about, according to their ufual cuftom; but man engaging againft man, each did all that lay in his power to unhorfe his enemy. Alexander loft threefcore of his guards in this attack. Hephæftion, Gœnus, and Menidas, were wounded in it, however he triumphed on this occafion, and all the Barbarians were cut to pieces, except fuch as forced their way through his fquadrons.

During this, news had been brought Mazæus that Darius was defeated; upon which, being greatly alarmed and dejected by the ill fuccefs of that monarch,

arch, though the advantage was entirely on his side, he ceased to charge the enemy, who were now in disorder, so briskly as before. Parmenio could not conceive how it came to pass, that the battle, which before was carried on so warmly, should slacken on a sudden: However, like an able commander, who seizes every advantage, and who employs his utmost endeavours to inspire his soldiers with fresh vigour, he observed to them, that the terror which spread throughout the whole army, was the forerunner of their defeat, and fired them with the notion how glorious it would be for them to put the last hand to the victory. Upon his exhortations, they recovered their former hopes and bravery; when, transformed into other men, they gave their horses the rein, and charged the enemy with so much fury, as threw them into the greatest disorder, and obliged them to fly. Alexander came up that instant, and overjoyed to find the scale turned in his favour, and the enemy entirely defeated, he renewed (in concert with Parmenio) the pursuit of Darius. He rode as far as Arbela, where he fancied he should come up with that monarch and all his baggage; but Darius had only just passed by it, and left his treasure a prey to the enemy, with his bow and shield.

Such was the success of this famous battle, which gave empire to the conqueror. According to Arrian, the Persians lost three hundred thousand men, besides those who were taken prisoners; which at least, is a proof that the loss was very great on their side. That of Alexander *(q)* was very inconsiderable, he not losing, according to the last mentioned
author,

(q) A. M 3674. *Ant. J. C.* 330.

author, twelve hundred men, moſt of whom were horſe. This engagement was fought in the month of * October, about the ſame time, two years before, that the battle of Iſſus was fought. As Gaugamela, in Aſſyria, the ſpot where the two armies engaged, was a ſmall place of very little note, this was called the battle of Arbela, that city being neareſt to the field of battle.

SECT. IX. *Alexander poſſeſſes himſelf of Arbela, Babylon, Suſa, Perſepolis ; and finds immenſe riches in thoſe cities. In the heat of drinking he ſets fire to the Palace of Perſepolis.*

ALEXANDER's firſt care, after his obtaining the victory, was to offer magnificent ſacrifices to the gods by way of thankſgiving. He afterwards rewarded ſuch as had ſignalized themſelves remarkably in battle ; beſtowed riches upon them, houſes, employments, and governments. But, being deſirous of expreſſing more particularly his gratitude to the Greeks, for having appointed him generaliſſimo againſt the Perſians, he gave order, for aboliſhing the ſeveral tyrannical inſtitutions that had ſtarted up in Greece ; that the cities ſhould be reſtored to their liberties, with all their rights and privileges.

Darius, after his defeat, having but very few attendants, had rode towards the river Lycus. After croſſing it, ſeveral adviſed him to break down the bridges,

* *The month called by the Greeks Boedromion, anſwers partly to our month of October.*

bridges, because the enemy pursued him. But he made this generous answer, "That life was not so dear to him, as to make him desire to preserve it by the destruction of so many thousands of his subjects and faithful allies, who, by that means, would be delivered up to the mercy of the enemy; that they had as much right to pass over this bridge as their sovereign, and consequently that it ought to be as open to them." After riding a great number of leagues full speed, he arrived at midnight at Arbela. From thence he fled towards Media, over the Armenian mountains, followed by a great number of the nobility, and a few of his guards. The reason of his going that way was, his supposing that Alexander would proceed towards Babylon and Susa, there to enjoy the fruits of his victory; besides, a numerous army could not pursue him by this road; whereas, in the other, horses and chariots might advance with great ease; not to mention that the soil was very fruitful.

A few days after Arbela surrendered to Alexander, who found in it a great quantity of furniture belonging to the crown, rich clothes, and other precious moveables, with four thousand talents (about 775,000l.) and all the riches of the army, which Darius had left there at his setting out against Alexander, as was before observed. But he was soon obliged to leave that place, because of the diseases that spread in his camp, occasioned by the infection of the dead bodies which covered all the field of battle. This prince advanced therefore over the plains towards Babylon, and, after four days march, arrived at Memnis, where, in a cave, is seen the celebrated fountain which throws out so vast a quantity

ry of bitumen, that, we are told, it was used as cement in building the walls of Babylon.

When Alexander was got near Babylon, Mazæus, who had retired thither after the battle of Arbela, surrendered himself, with his children, who were grown up, and gave the city into his hands. The king was very well pleased with his arrival; for he would have met with great difficulties in besieging a city of such importance, and so well provided with every thing. Besides his being a person of great quality, and very brave, he had also acquired great honour in the last battle; and others might have been prompted, from the example he set them, to imitate him. Alexander entered the city at the head of his whole army, as if he had been marching to a battle. The walls of Babylon were lined with people, notwithstanding the greatest part of the citizens were gone out before, from the impatient desire they had to see their new sovereign, whose renown had far outstriped his march. Bagophanes, governor of the fortress, and guardian of the treasure, unwilling to discover less zeal than Mazæus, strewed the streets with flowers, and raised on both sides of the way silver alters, which smoaked not only with frankincense, but the most fragrant perfumes of every kind. Last of all came the presents which were to be made the king, viz. herds of cattle, and a great number of horses; as also lions and panthers, which were carried in cages. After these the Magi walked, singing hymns after the manner of their country; then the Chaldeans accompanied by the Babylonish soothsayers and musicians: it was customary for the latter to sing the praises of their kings to their instruments; and the Chaldeans to observe the motion

of

of the planets, and the viciffitude of feafons. The rear was brought up by the Babylonifh cavalry, which both men and horfes were fo fumptuous, that imagination can fcarce reach their magnificence. The king caufed the people to walk after his infantry, and himfelf, furrounded with his guards, and feated on a chariot, entered the city; and from thence rode to the palace, as in a kind of triumph. The next day he took a view of all Darius's money and moveables. Of the monies he found in Babylon, he gave, by way of extraordinary recompence, to each Macedonian horfe-men, fix minæ, (about fifteen pounds;) to each mercenary horfe-man two minæ, (about five pounds;) to every Macedonian foot foldier two minæ; and to every one of the reft two months of their ordinary pay. He gave orders, purfuant to the advice of the Magi, with whom he had feveral conferences, for the rebuilding the temples which Xerxes had demolifhed; and, among others, that of Belus, who was in greater veneration at Babylon than any other deity. He gave the government of the province to Mazæus, and the command of the forces he left there to Apollodorus of Amphipolis.

Alexander, in the midft of the hurry and tumult of war, ftill preferved a love for the fciences. He ufed often to converfe with the Chaldeans, who had always applied themfelves to the ftudy of aftronomy from its origin, and gained great fame by their knowledge in it. They prefented him with aftronomical obfervations taken by their predeceffors during the fpace of 1903 years, which confequently went as far backward as the age of Nimrod.

The

The king resided longer in Babylon than he had done in any other city, which was of great prejudice to the discipline of his forces. The people, even from a religious motive, abandoned themselves to pleasures, to voluptuousness, and to the most infamous excesses; nor did ladies, though of the highest quality, observe any decorum, or show the least reserve in their immoral actions, but gloried therein, so far from endeavouring to conceal them, or blushing at their enormity. It must be confessed, that this army of soldiers, which had triumphed over Asia, after having thus enervated themselves, and rioted, as it were in the sloth and luxury of the city of Babylon, for thirty-four days together, would have been scarce able to complete their exploits, had they been opposed by an enemy. But, as they were re-inforced from time to time, these irregularities were not so visible; for Amyntas brought six thousand foot and five hundred Macedonian horse, which were sent by Antipater; and six hundred Thracian horse, with three thousand five hundred foot of the same nation; besides four thousand mercenaries from Peloponnesus, with near four hundred horses.

The above-mentioned Amyntas had also brought the king fifty Macedonian youths, sons to noblemen of the highest quality in the country, to serve as his guards. The youths in question waited upon him at table, brought him his horses when in the field, attended upon him in parties of hunting, and kept guard at the door of his apartment by turns; and these were the first steps to the highest employments both in the army and the State.

After Alexander had left Babylon he marched towards Susa, where he arrived in twenty days. As he came near it, Abutites, governor of the province, sent his son to meet him, with a promise to surrender the city into his hands; whether he was prompted to this from his own inclination, or did it in obedience to the orders of Darius, to amuse Alexander with the hopes of plunder, the king gave this young nobleman a very gracious reception, who attended him as far as the river Choaspes, the waters of which are so famous, upon account of their exquisite taste. *(m)* The kings of Persia never drank of any other; and whithersoever they went a quantity of it, after having been put over the fire, was always carried after them in silver vases. It was here Abutites came to wait upon him, bringing presents worthy of a king; among which were dromedaries of incredible swiftness, and twelve elephants which Darius had sent for from India. Being come into the city, he took immense sums out of the treasury, with fifty thousand *talents of silver in ore and ingots, besides moveables, and a thousand other things of infinite value. This wealth was the produce of the exactions imposed for several centuries upon the common people, from whose sweat and poverty immense revenues were raised. The Persian monarchs fancied they had amassed them for their children and posterity; but, in one hour, they fell into the hands of a foreign king, who was able to make a right use of them; for Alexander seemed to be merely the guardian or trustee of the immense riches which he found hoarded up in Persia; and applied them to no other use than the rewarding of merit and courage.

Among

---

* *About seven millions five hundred thousand pounds.*

Among other things, there was found * five thousand quintals of Hermione † purple, the finest in the world, which had been treasuring up there during the space of one hundred and ninety years; notwithstanding which, its beauty and lustre was no ways diminished.

Here likewise was found part of the rarities which Xerxes had brought from Greece; and, among others, the brazen statues of Harmodius and Aristogiton, which Alexander sent afterwards to Athens, where they were standing in Arrian's time.

The king being resolved to march into Persia, appointed Archilaus governor of the city of Susa, with a garrison of three thousand men; Mazarus, one of the lords of his court, was made governor of the citadel, with a thousand Macedonian soldiers, who could not follow him by reason of their great age. He gave the government of Susiana to Abutites.

He left Darius's mother and children in Susa, and having received from Macedonia a great quantity of purple stuffs and rich habits, made after the fashion of the country, he presented them to Sysigambis, together with the artificers who had wrought them; for he paid her every kind of honour, and loved her as tenderly as if she had been his mother. He likewise commanded the messengers to tell her, that in case she fancied those stuffs, she might make her grandchildren learn the art of weaving them, by way of amusement; and to give them as presents to whomsoever they should think proper. At these words, the

---

* *The reader will have an idea of the prodigious value of this, when he is told, that this purple was sold at the rate of an hundred livres a pound. The quintal is an hundred weight of Paris.*

† *Hermione was a city of Argolis, where the best purple was died.*

the tears which fell from her eyes shewed but too evidently how greatly she was displeased at these gifts; the working in wool being considered by the Persian women as the highest ignominy. Those who carried these presents having told the king that Sysigambis was very much dissatisfied, he thought himself obliged to make an apology for what he had done, and administer some consolation to her. Accordingly, he paid her a visit, when he spoke thus: "Mother, the stuff in which you see me clothed, "was not only a gift of my sisters, but wrought by "their fingers. Hence I beg you to believe, that "the custom of my country misled me; and do not "consider that as an insult, which was owing en- "tirely to ignorance." I believe I have not, as "yet, done any thing which I knew interfered with "your manners and customs. I was told, that "among the Persians, it was a sort of crime for a "son to seat himself in his mother's presence, with- "out first obtaining her leave. You are sensible "how cautious I have always been in this particu- "lar; and that I never sit down, till you have first "laid your commands upon me to do so. And "every time that you was going to fall prostrate be- "fore me, I only ask you, whether I should suffer "it? As the highest testimony of the veneration I "have for you, I always called you by the tender "name of mother, though this belongs properly to "Olympias only, to whom I owe my birth."

Alexander, having taken his leave of Sysigambis, who now was extremely well satisfied, arrived on the banks of a river, called by the inhabitants Pasi Tigris.‡ Having crossed it with nine thousand foot, and

---

‡ *This river differs from the Tigris.*

and three thousand horse, consisting of Agrians, as well as Grecian mercenaries, and a reinforcement of three thousand Thracians, he entered the country of the Uxii. This region lies near Susa, and extends to the frontiers of Persia; a narrow pass only lying between it and Susiana. Medathes commanded this province. This man was not a timeserver, nor a follower of fortune; but, faithful to his sovereign, he resolved to hold out to the last extremity; and, for this purpose, had withdrawn into his own city, which stood in the midst of craggy rocks, and was surrounded with precipices. Having been forced from thence, he retired into the citadel, whence the besieged sent thirty deputies to Alexander, to sue for quarter; which they obtained, at last, by the intercession of Sysigambis. The king not only pardoned Madathes, who was a near relation of that princess, but likewise set all the captives, and those who had surrendered themselves, at liberty; permitted them to enjoy their several rights and privileges; would not suffer the city to be plundered, but let them plough their lands without paying any tax or tribute. Could Sysigambis have possibly obtained more from her own son on this occasion, had he been the victor?

The Uxii being subdued, Alexander gave part of his army to Parmenio, and commanded him to march it through the plain; whilst himself at the head of his light armed troops, crossed the mountains, which extend as far as Persia. The fifth day he arrived at the pass of Susa. Ariobarzanes, with four thousand foot and seven hundred horse, had taken possession of those rocks which were craggy on all sides, and posted the Barbarians at the summit, out of the reach

reach of arrows. He also had built a wall in those passes, and encamped his forces under it. As soon as Alexander advanced, in order to attack him, the Barbarians rolled from the top of the mountains, stones of a prodigious size, which falling from rock to rock, rushed forward with the greater violence, and at once crushed to pieces whole bands of soldiers. The king, being very much terrified at this sight, commanded a retreat to be sounded; and it was with the utmost grief he saw himself not only stopped at this pass, but deprived of all hopes of ever being able to force it.

Whilst he was revolving these gloomy thoughts, a Grecian prisoner surrendered himself to Alexander, with a promise to conduct him to the top of the mountain by another way. The king accepted of the offer, when, leaving the superintendance of the camp and of the army to Craterus, he commanded him to cause a great number of fires to be lighted, in order that the Barbarians might thereby be more strongly induced to believe, that Alexander was there in person. After this, taking some chosen troops with him, he set out, going through all the by-ways, as his guide directed. But, besides that these paths were very craggy, and the rocks so slippery, that their feet would scarce stand upon them; the soldiers were also very much distressed by the snows which the winds had brought together, and which were so high, that the men fell into them, as into so many ditches; and when their comrades endeavoured to draw them out they themselves would likewise sink into them, not to mention that their fears were greatly increased by the horrors of the night, by their being in an unknown country, and conducted by a

guide,

guide, whose fidelity was doubtful. After having gone through a great number of difficulties and dangers, they at last got to the top of the mountain. Then going down, they discovered the enemy's corps-de-garde, and appeared behind them, sword in hand, at a time when they least expected it. Such as made the least defence, who were but few, were cut to pieces; by which means the cries of the dying on one side, and on the other the fright of those who were flying to their main body, spread so great a terror, that they fled, without striking a blow. At this noise Craterus advanced, as Alexander had commanded at his going away, and seized the pass, which till then had resisted his attacks; and, at the same time, Philotus advanced forwards by another way, with Amyntas, Cœnus, and Polysperchon, and broke quite through the Barbarians, who now were attacked on every side. The greatest part of them were cut to pieces, and those who fled, fell into precipices. Ariobarzanes, with part of the cavalry, escaped by flying over the mountains.

Alexander, from an effect of the good fortune, which constantly attended him in all his undertakings, having extricated himself happily out of the danger to which he was so lately exposed, marched immediately towards Persia. Being on the road, he received letters from Tiridates, governor of Persepolis, which informed him, that the inhabitants of that city, upon the report of his advancing towards him, were determined to plunder Darius's treasures, with which he was intrusted, and therefore that it was necessary for him to make all the haste imaginable to seize them himself; that he had only the * Araxes to cross,

---

* *This is not the same river with that in Armenia.*

cross, after which the road was smooth and easy. Alexander, upon this news, leaving his infantry behind, marched the whole night at the head of his cavalry, who were very much harrassed by the length and swiftness of this march, and passed the Araxes on a bridge, which, by his order, had been built some days before.

But, as he drew near the city, he perceived a large body of men, who exhibited a memorable example of the greatest misery. These were about four thousand Greeks, very far advanced in years, who, having been made prisoners of war, had suffered all the torments which the Persian tyranny could inflict. The hands of some had been cut off, the feet of others; and others again had lost their noses and ears: After which, having impressed, by fire, barbarous characters on their faces, they had the inhumanity to keep them as so many laughing-stocks, with which they used perpetually. They appeared like so many shadows, rather than like men; speech being almost the only thing by which they were known to be such. Alexander could not refrain from tears at this sight; and, as they unanimously besought him to commiserate their condition, he bid them with the utmost tenderness, not to despond, and assured them, that they should again see their wives and country. This proposal, which one might suppose should naturally have filled them with joy, perplexed them very much, various opinions arising on that occasion, " How " will it be possible (said some of them) for us to " appear publickly before all Greece, in the dread- " ful condition to which we are reduced; a condition " still more shameful than dissatisfactory? The best " way to bear misery is to conceal it; and no coun-
" try

"try is so sweet to the wretched, as solitude, and an oblivion of their past calamities. Besides, how will it be possible for us to undertake so long a journey? Driven to a great distance from Europe, banished to the most remote parts of the east, worn out with age, and most of our limbs maimed, can we pretend to undergo fatigues, which have even wearied a triumphant army? The only thing that now remains for us, is to hide our misery, and to end our days among those, who are already so accustomed to our misfortunes." Others, in whom the love of their country extinguished all other sentiments, represented, "That the gods offered them what they should not even have dared to wish, viz. their country, their wives, their children, and all those things for whose sake men are fond of life, and despise death. That they had long enough borne the sad yoke of slavery; and that nothing happier could present itself than their being indulged the bliss of going at last to breathe their native air, to resume their ancient manners, laws, and sacrifices, and to die in presence of their wives and children."

However, the former opinion prevailed; and accordingly they besought the king to permit them to continue in a country where they had spent so many years. He granted their request, and presented each of them* three thousand drachmas; five men's suits of clothes, and the same number for women; two couple of oxen to plough their lands, and corn to sow them. He commanded the governor of the province not to suffer them to be molested in any manner, and ordered that they should be free from taxes

* *About one hundred and fifty pounds.*

taxes and tributes of every kind. Such behaviour as this was truly royal.

Alexander having called together, the next day, the generals of his army, represented to them, " That no city in the world had ever been more fa- " tal to the Greeks than Persepolis, the ancient resi- " dence of the Persian monarchs, and the capital of " their empire. For that it was from thence all " those mighty armies poured, which had overflow- " ed Greece ; and whence Darius, and afterwards " Xerxes, had carried the firebrand of the most ac- " cursed war, which had laid waste all Europe ; and " therefore that it was incumbent on them to re- " venge the manes of their ancestors." It was already abandoned by the Persians, who all fled separately as fear drove them. Alexander entered it with his phalanx, when the victorious soldiers soon met with riches sufficient to satiate their avarice, and immediately cut to pieces all those who still remained in the city. However, the king soon put an end to the massacre, and published an order, by which his his soldiers were forbid to violate the chastity of the women. Alexander had before possessed himself, either by force or capitulation, of a great number of incredible rich cities ; but all this was a trifle compared to the treasures he found here. The Barbarians had laid up at Persepolis, as in a store-house, all the wealth of Persia. Gold and silver were never seen here but in heaps, not to mention the clothes and furniture of inestimable value ; for this was the seat of luxury. There was found in the treasury one hundred and twenty thousand talents *, which were designed to defray the expence of the war. To this prodigious

---

* About eighteen millions sterling.

prodigious sum, he added † six thousand talents, taken from Pesagarda. This was a city which Cyrus had built, wherein the kings of Persia used to be crowned.

During Alexander's stay in Persepolis, a little before he set out upon his march against Darius, he entertained his friends at a banquet, at which the guests drank to excess. Among the women, who were admitted to it masked, was Thais the courtesan, a native of Attica, and at that time mistress to Ptolemy, who afterwards was king of Egypt. About the end of the feast, during which she had studiously endeavoured to praise the king in the most artful and delicate manner (a stratagem too often practised by women of that character) she said, with a gay tone of voice, "That it would be matter of inexpressible
" joy to her were she permitted (masked as she then
" was, and in order to end this festival nobly) to
" burn the magnificent palace of Xerxes, who had
" burned Athens; and set it on fire with her own
" hand, in order that it might be said in all parts of
" the world, that the women, who had followed
" Alexander in his expedition to Asia, had taken
" much better vengeance of the Persians, for the
" many calamities they had brought upon the Grecians, than all the generals who had fought for
" them both by sea and land." All the guests applauded the discourse; when immediately the king rose from table (his head being crowned with flowers) and taking a torch in his hand, he advanced forward to execute this mighty exploit. The whole company follow him, breaking into loud acclamations, and afterwards singing and dancing, they sur-

† *About nine hundred thousand pounds.*

round

round the palace. All the rest of the Macedonians, at this noise, ran in crouds, with lighted tapers, and set fire to every part of it. However, Alexander was sorry, not long after, for what he had done; and thereupon gave orders for extinguishing the fire, but it was too late.

SECT. X. *Darius leaves Ecbatana. He is betrayed and put in chains by Bessus, governor of Bactria. The latter, upon Alexander's advancing towards him, flies, after having covered Darius with wounds, who expires a few moments before Alexander's arrival. He sends his corps to Sysigambis.*

ALEXANDER, after he had taken rsepolis and Passagarda, was resolved to pursue Darius, who was arrived by this time at Ecbatana, the capital of Media. There remained still with this fugitive prince thirty thousand foot, among whom were four thousand Greeks, who were faithful to him to the last. Besides these he had four thousand slingers, and upwards of three thousand cavalry, most of them commanded by Bessus, governor of Bactria. Darius marched his forces a little out of the common road, having ordered his baggage to go before them; then assembling his principal officers, he spoke to them as follows: "Dear companions, among so many
" thousand men who composed my army, you only
" have not abandoned me during the whole course of
" my ill fortune; and in a little time, nothing but
" your fidelity and constancy will be able to make
" me fancy myself a king. Deserters and traitors

" now govern my cities; not that they are thought
" worthy of the honour beftowed on them, but re-
" wards are given them only in the view of tempting
" you, and to ftagger your perfeverance. You
" ftill chofe to follow my fortune rather than that of
" the conqueror, for which you certainly have merited
" a recompence from the gods; and I do not doubt
" but they will prove beneficent towards you; in
" cafe that power is denied me. With fuch fold-
" iers and officers I would brave, without the leaft
" dread, the enemy, how formidable foever he may
" be. What! would any one have me furrender
" myfelf up to the mercy of the conqueror, and ex-
" pect from him, as a reward of my bafenefs and
" meannefs of fpirit, the government of fome pro-
" vince which he may condefcend to leave me?
" No—it never fhall be in the power of any man,
" either to take away, or fix upon my head the dia-
" dem I wear; the fame hour fhall put a period to
" reign and life. If you have all the fame courage
" and refolution, which I can no ways doubt, I af-
" fure myfelf that you fhall retain your liberty, and
" not be expofed to the pride and infults of the Ma-
" cedonians. You have in your hands the means,
" either to revenge or terminate all your evils."
Having ended this fpeech, the whole body of foldiers replied with fhouts, that they were ready to follow him whitherfoever he fhould go, and would fhed
the laft drop of their blood in his defence.

Such was the refolution of the foldiery; but Nabarzanes, one of the greateft lords of Perfia, and
general of the horfe, had confpired with Beffus,
general of the Bactrians, to commit the blackeft of
all crimes, and that was to feize upon the perfon of

the

the king, and lay him in chains; which they might easily do, as each of them had a great number of soldiers under his command. Their design was, if Alexander should pursue them, to secure themselves, by giving up Darius alive into his hands; and, in case they escaped, to murther that prince, and afterwards usurp his crown, and begin a new war. These traitors soon won over the troops, by representing to them, that they were going to their destruction; that they would soon be crushed under the ruins of an empire, which was just ready to fall; at the same time that Bractriana was open to them, and offered them immense riches. Though these practices were carried on very secretly, they came however to the ear of Darius, who could not believe them. Patron, who commanded the Greeks, intreated him, but in vain, to pitch his tent among them, and to trust the guard of his person to men on whose fidelity he might depend. Darius could not prevail with himself to put so great an affront upon the Persians, and therefore made this answer: " That it would be a less af-
" fliction to him to be deceived by, than to condemn
" them. That he would suffer the worst of evils
" amidst those of his own nation, rather than seek
" for security among strangers, how faithful and af-
" fectionate soever he might believe them: and that
" he could not but die too late, in case the Persian
" soldiers thought him unworthy of life." It was not long before Darius experienced the truth of this counsel: for the traitors seized him, bound him in chains of gold, by way of honour, as he was a king, and then laying him in a covered chariot, they set towards Bactriana.

Alexander

Alexander being arrived at Ecbatana, was informed that Darius had left that city five days before. He then commanded Parmenio to lay up all the treasures of Persia, in the castle of Ecbatana, under a strong guard which he left there. According to Strabo, these treasures amounted to an hundred and eighty thousand talents (about twenty-seven millions sterling ;) and, according to Justin, to ten talents more, (about fifteen hundred thousand pounds.) He ordered him to march afterwards towards Hyrcania, by the country of the Cadusians, with the Thracians, the foreigners, and the rest of the cavalry, the royal companies excepted. He sent orders to Clitus, who stayed behind in Susa, where he fell sick, that as soon as he was arrived at Ecbatana, he should take the forces which were left in that city, and come to him in Parthia.

Alexander, with the rest of his army, pursued Darius, and arrived the eleventh day at Rhaga, which is a long day's journey from the Caspian straits; but Darius had already passed through them. Alexander now despairing to overtake him, what dispatch soever he might make, stayed there five days to rest his forces. He then marched against the Parthians, and that day pitched his camp near the Caspian straits, and passed them the next. News was soon brought him, that Darius had been seized by the traitors, that Bessus had caused him to be drawn in a chariot, and had sent the unhappy monarch before, in order to be the surer of his person; that the whole army obeyed that wretch. Artabazus and the Greeks excepted, who not having a soul base enough to consent to so abominable a deed, and being too weak to prevent it, had therefore left the high road, and marched towards the mountains. This

This was a fresh motive for him to hasten his march. The Barbarians, at his arrival, were seized with dread, though the match would not have been equal, had Bessus been as resolute for fighting, as for putting in execution the detestable act above-mentioned; for his troops exceeded the enemy both in number and strength, and were all cool and ready for the combat; whereas Alexander's troops were quite fatigued with the length of their march. But the name and reputation of Alexander (a motive all powerful in war) filled them with such prodigious terror, that they all fled. Bessus and his accomplices being come up with Darius, they requested him to mount his horse, and fly from the enemy, but he replied, that the gods were ready to revenge the evils he had suffered; and beseeching Alexander to do him justice, he refused to follow a band of traitors. At these words they fell into such a fury, that all threw their darts at him, and left him covered with wounds. After having perpetrated this horrid crime, they separated, in order to leave different footsteps of their flight, and thereby elude the pursuit of the enemy, in case he should follow them; or at least oblige him to divide his forces. Nabarzanes took the way of Hyrcania, and Bessus that of Bactriana, both being followed by a very few horse-men; and, as the Barbarians were by this means destitute of leaders, they dispersed themselves up and down, as fear or hope directed their steps.

After searching about in different places, Darius was at last found in a solitude, his body run through with spears, lying in a chariot, and drawing near his end. However, he had strength enough before he died to call for drink, which a Macedonian, Polyf-
tratus

tratus by name, brought him. He had a Perſian priſoner, whom he employed as his interpreter. Darius, after drinking the liquor that had been given him, turned to the Macedonian, and ſaid, "That
" in the deplorable ſtate to which he was reduced,
" he however ſhould have the comfort to ſpeak to
" one who could underſtand him, and that his laſt words
" would not be loſt. He therefore charged him to
" tell Alexander, that he died in his debt, though
" he had never obliged him. That he gave him a
" multitude of thanks for the great humanity he
" had exerciſed towards his mother, his wife,
" and his children, whoſe lives he had not only
" ſpared, but reſtored them to their former ſplen-
" dour. That he beſought the gods to give victory
" to his arms, and make him monarch of the uni-
" verſe. That he thought he need not intreat him to
" revenge the execrable murder committed on his
" perſon, as this was the common cauſe of kings."
After this, taking Polyſtratus' by the hand,
" Give him (ſaid he) thy hand, as I give thee
" mine, and carry him, in my name, the only pledge,
" I am able to give of my gratitude and affection."
Saying theſe words, he breathed his laſt. Alexander coming up a moment after, and ſeeing Darius's body, he wept bitterly; and by the ſtrongeſt teſtimonies of affection that could be given him, proved how intimately he was affected with the unhappineſs of a prince who deſerved a better fate. He immediately pulled off his military cloak, and threw it on Darius's body; then cauſing it to be embalmed, and his coffin to be adorned with a royal magnificence, he ſent it to Syſigambis, in order that it might be interred with the honours uſually paid to the deceaſed

ceased Persian monarchs, and to be entombed with his ancestors.

Thus died Darius, the third year of the 112th Olympiad, at about fifty years of age, six of which he had reigned. He was a gentle and pacific prince; his reign had been unsullied with injustice or cruelty, which was owing either to his natural lenity, or to his not having had an opportunity of acting otherwise, from the perpetual war he had carried on against Alexander all the time he had set upon the throne. In him the Persian empire ended, after having existed two hundred and nine years, computing from the beginning to the reign of Cyrus the Great (the founder of it) under thirteen kings, viz. Cyrus, Cambyses, Smerdis Magus, Darius, son of Hystaspis, Xerxes I. Artaxerxes Longimanus, Xerxes II. Sogdianus, Darius Notus, Artaxerxes Memnon, Artaxerxes Ochus, Arses, and Darius Codomanus.

SECT. XI. *Lacedemonia revolts from the Macedonians, with almost all Peloponnesus. Antipater marches out upon this occasion, defeats the enemy in a battle, in which Agis is killed. Alexander marches against Bessus. Thalestris, queen of the Amazons, comes to visit him from a far country. Alexander, at his return from Parthia, abandons himself to pleasure and excess. He continues his march towards Bessus. A pretended conspiracy of Philotas against the king. He and Parmenio his father, are put to death. Alexander subdues several nations. He at last arrives in Bactriana, whither Bessus is brought to him.*

WHILST

WHILST things passed in Asia, as we have seen, some tumults broke out in Greece and Macedonia. Memnon, whom Alexander had sent into Thrace, having revolted there, and thereby drawn the forces of Antipater on that side; the Lacedæmonians thought this a proper opportunity to throw off the Macedonian yoke, and engaged almost all Peloponessus in their design. Upon this news, Antipater, after having settled to the best of his power the affairs of Thrace, returned with the utmost expedition into Greece, whence he immediately dispatched courtiers, in order to give Alexander an account of these several transactions. As soon as Antipater was come up with the enemy, he resolved to venture a battle. The Lacedæmonian army consisted of no more than twenty thousand foot, and two thousand horse, under the command of Agis their king; whereas that of Antipater was twice that number. Agis, in order to make the superiority of numbers of no effect, had made choice of a narrow spot of ground. The battle began with great vigour, each party endeavouring to signalise themselves in an extraordinary manner, for the honour of their respective countries; the one fired with the remembrance of their pristine glory, and the other animated by their present greatness, fought with equal courage; the Lacedæmonians for liberty, and the Macedonians for empire. So long as the armies continued on the spot where the battle began, Agis had the advantage; but Antipater, by pretending to fly, drew the enemy into the plains; after which, extending his whole army, he gained a superiority, and made a proper use of his advantage. Agis was distinguished by his suit of armour, his noble mein,

and

and still more so by his valour. The battle was hottest round his person, and he himself performed the most astonishing acts of bravery. At last, after having been wounded in several parts of his body, his soldiers laying him upon his shield, carried him off. However, this did not damp his courage, for having seized an advantageous post where they kept close in their ranks, they resisted with great vigour, the attacks of the enemy. After having withstood them a long time, the Lacedæmonians began to give ground, being scarce able to hold their arms, which were all covered with sweat; they afterwards retired very fast, and at last ran quite away. The king seeing himself closely pursued, still made some efforts, notwithstanding the weak condition to which he was reduced, in order to oppose the enemy. Intrepid and invincible to the last, oppressed by numbers, he died sword in hand.

In this engagement upwards of three thousand Lacedemonians lost their lives, and a thousand Macedonians at most; but very few of the latter returned home unwounded. This victory not only ruined the power of Sparta and its allies, but also the hopes of those who only waited the issue of this war, to declare themselves. Antipater immediately sent the news of this success to Alexander: but, like an experienced courtier, he drew up the account of it in the most modest and circumspect terms; in such as were best adapted to diminish the lustre of a victory which might expose him to envy. He was sensible, that Alexander's delicacy, with regard to honor; was so very great, that he looked upon the glory which another person obtained, as a diminution of his own. And, indeed he could not forbear, when this news was

was brought him, to let drop fome words which difcovered his jealoufy. Antipater did not dare to difpofe of any thing by his own private authority, and only gave the Lacedemonians leave to fend an embaffy to the king, in order that they themfelves might tell him the ill fuccefs they had met with. Alexander pardoned them, fome of thofe who had occafioned the revolt excepted, and thefe he punifhed.

Darius's death did not hinder Alexander from purfuing Beffus, who had withdrawn in Bactriana, where he had affumed the title of king, by the name of Artaxerxes. But, finding at laft that it would be impoffible for him to come up with him, returned into Parthia; and refting his troops fome days in Hetacompylos, commanded provifions of all forts to be brought thither.

During his ftay there, a report prevailed throughout the whole army, that the king, content with the conquefts he had atchieved, was preparing to return into Macedonia. That very inftant the foldiers, as if a fignal had been made for their fetting out, ran like madmen to their tents, began to pack up their baggage, load the waggons with the utmoft difpatch and fill the whole camp with noife and tumult. Alexander was foon informed of this, when terrified at the diforder, he fummoned the officers to his tent, where, with tears in his eyes, he complained, that in the midft of fo glorious a career, he was ftopped on a fudden, and forced to return back into his own country, rather like one who had been overcome, than as a conqueror. The officers comforted him, by reprefenting, that this fudden motion was a mere fally, and a tranfient guft of paffion, which would not be attended with any ill confequences; and afsured him, that the soldiers, to a man, would obey him, provided he would addrefs himfelf to them in tender expreffions. He promifed to do it. The circumftance which had given occafion to this falfe report, was, his having difbanded fome Grecian foldiers, after rewarding them in a very bountiful manner; fo that the Macedonians imagined they alfo were to fight no more.

Alexander having fummoned the army, made the following fpeech. "I am not furprifed, O foldiers, " if, after the mighty things we have hitherto per‑ " formed, you fhould be fatiated with glory, and " have no other views but eafe and repofe. I will " not now enumerate the various nations we have " conquered. We have fubdued more provinces " than others have cities. Could I perfuade myfelf, " that our conquefts were well fecured, over nations " who were fo foon overcome, I would think as you " do (for I will not diffemble my thoughts) and " would make all the hafte imaginable to revifit my " houfehold gods, my mother, my fifters, and my " fubjects, and enjoy in the midft of my country the " glory I have acquired in concert with you. But " this glory will all vanifh very foon, if we do not " put the laft hand to the work. Do you imagine, " that fo many nations, accuftomed to other fover‑ " eigns, and who have no manner of fimilitude to us " either in their religion, manners, or language, were " entirely fubdued the moment they were conquer‑ " ed; and that they will not take up arms, in cafe " we return back with fo much precipitation? What " will become of the reft who ftill remain uncon‑ " quered? How! fhall we leave our victory imper‑ " fect, merely for want of courage! But that which
" touches

"touches me much more; shall we suffer the detestable crime of Bessus to go unpunished? Can you bear to see the sceptre of Darius in the sanguinary hands of that monster, who, after having loaded him with chains, as a captive, at last assassinated his sovereign, in order to deprive us of the glory of saving him? As for myself, I shall not be easy till I see that infamous wretch hanging on a gibbet, there to pay, to all kings and nations of the earth, the just punishment due to his execrable crime. I do not know whether I am mistaken; but methinks I read his sentence of death in your countenances; and that the anger which sparkles in your eyes, declares you will soon imbrue your hands in that traitor's blood."

The soldiers would not suffer Alexander to proceed; but clapping their hands, they all cried aloud, that they were ready to follow wherever he should lead them. All the speeches of this prince generally produced this effect. In how desponding a condition soever they might be, one single word from him revived their courage in an instant, and inspired them with that martial alacrity and ardour, which appeared always in his face. The king, taking advantage of this favourable disposition of the whole army, crossed Parthia, and in three days arrived on the frontiers of Hyrcania, which submitted to his arms. He afterwards subdued the Mardi, the Arii, the Drangæ, the Arachosii, and the several other nations, into which his army marched, with greater speed than people generally travel. He frequently would pursue an enemy for whole days and nights together, almost without suffering his troops to take any rest. By this prodigious rapidity, he came unawares upon

nations

nations who thought him at a great diſtance, and ſubdued them before they had time to put themſelves in a poſture of defence. Under this image Daniel the prophet ſhadowed Alexander many ages before his birth, by repreſenting him as a panther, a leopard, and a goat, who ruſhed forward with ſo much ſwitneſs, that his feet ſeemed not to touch the ground.

Nabarzanes, one of Beſſus's accomplices, who had written before to Alexander, came and ſurrendered himſelf, upon promiſe of a pardon, when he heard that he was arrived at Zadracarta, the capital of Hyrcania; and, among other preſents, brought him Bagoas the eunuch, who afterwards gained as great an aſcendant over Alexander, as before over Darius.

At the ſame time arrived Thaleſtris, queen of the Amazons. A violent deſire of ſeeing Alexander had prompted that princeſs to leave her dominions, and travel through a great number of countries to gratify her curioſity. Being come pretty near his camp, ſhe ſent word that a queen was come to viſit him; and that ſhe had a prodigious inclination to cultivate his acquaintance, and accordingly was arrived within a little diſtance from that place. Alexander having returned her a favorable anſwer, ſhe commanded her train to ſtop, and herſelf came forward with three hundred women; and the moment ſhe perceived the king, ſhe leaped from her horſe, having two lances in her right hand. The dreſs the Amazons uſed to wear, did not quite cover the body; for their boſom being uncovered on the left ſide, every other part of their body was hid; their gowns being tucked up with a knot, and ſo deſcended no farther than the knee. They preſerved their right breaſt to ſuckle their female offspring, but uſed to burn the left,

left, that they might be the better enabled to bend the bow and throw the dart, whence they were called *Amazons.

Thaleſtris looked upon the king without diſcovering the leaſt ſign of admiration, and ſurveying him attentively, did not think his ſtature anſwerable to his fame; for the Barbarians are very much ſtruck with a majeſtic air, and think thoſe only capable of mighty atchievements, on whom nature has beſtowed bodily advantages. She did not ſcruple to tell him, that the chief motive of her journey, was to have poſterity by him; adding, that ſhe was worthy of giving heirs to his empire. Alexander, upon this requeſt, was obliged to make ſome ſtay in this place; after which Thaleſtris returned to her kingdom, and the king into the province inhabited by the Parthians. This ſtory, and whatever is related of the Amazons, is looked upon by ſome very judicious authors, entirely fabulous.

Alexander devoted himſelf afterwards wholly to his paſſions, changing into pride and debauch the moderation and continence for which he had hitherto been ſo greatly admired; virtues ſo very neceſſary in an exalted ſtation of life, and in the midſt of a ſeries of proſperities. He now was no longer the ſame man. Though he was invincible, with regard to the dangers and toils of war, he was far otherwiſe with reſpect to the charms of eaſe. The inſtant he enjoyed a little repoſe, he abandoned himſelf to ſenſuality; and he, whom the arms of the Perſians could not conquer, fell a victim to their vices. Nothing was now to be ſeen but games, parties of pleaſures, women, and exceſſive feaſting, in which he uſed to revel

* *This is a Greek word ſignifying, without breaſts.*

revel whole days and nights. Not satisfied with the buffoons, and the performers on inftrumental mufic, whom he had brought with him out of Greece, he obliged the captive women, whom he carried along with him, to fing fongs after the manner of their country. He happened, among thefe women, to perceive one who appeared in deeper affliction than the reft, and who, by a modeft, and at the fame time a noble confufion, difcovered a greater reluctance than the others, to appear in publick. She was a perfect beauty, which was very much heightened by her bafhfulnefs, whilft fhe threw her eyes to the ground, and did all in her power to conceal her face. The king foon imagined by her air and mien that fhe was not of vulgar birth; and enquiring himfelf into it, the lady anfwered, that fhe was grand-daughter to Ochus, who not long before had fwayed the Perfian fceptre, and daughter of his fon; that fhe had married Hvftafpes, who was related to Darius, and general of a great army. Alexander being touched with compaffion, when he heard the unhappy fate of a princefs of the blood royal, and the fad condition to which fhe was reduced, not only gave her liberty, but returned all her poffeffions; and caufed her hufband to be fought for, in order that fhe might be reftored him.

This prince was naturally of fo tender and humane a difpofition, as made him fenfible of the affliction of perfons in the loweft condition. A poor Macedonian was one day leading before him a mule, laden with gold for the king's ufe; the beaft being fo tired that he was not able either to go on or fuftain the load, the mule-driver took it up and carried, but with great difficulty, a confiderable way. Alexander, feeing seeing him juft finking under his burthen, and going to throw it on the ground, in order to eafe himfelf, cried out, Friend, do not be weary yet; try and carry it quite through to thy tent, for it is all thy own.

Alexander, in a very difficult march through barren places, at the head of a fmall body of horfe, when he purfued Darius, met fome Macedonians who were carrying water in goat-fkins upon mules. Thefe Macedonians perceiving their *ce* was almoft parched with thirft, occafioned by the raging heat (the fun being then at the meridian) immediately filled a helmet with water, and were running to prefent him with it : Alexander afking to whom they were carrying all that water, they replied, We are going to carry it to our children;. but do not let your majefty be uneafy, for if your life is but faved, we fhall get children enough, in cafe we fhould lofe thefe. At thefe words Alexander takes the helmet, and looking quite round him, he faw all his horfemen hanging down their heads, and with eyes fixed earneftly on the liquor he held, fwallow it, as it were, with their glances; upon which he returned it, with thanks to thofe who offered it him, and did not drink fo much as a fingle drop, but cried, There is not enough for my whole company; and fhould I drink alone, it would make the reft be thirftier, and they will quite die away. The officers, who were on horfeback round him, ftruck in the moft fenfible manner with his wonderful temperance and magnanimity, intreated him, with fhouts, to carry them wherever he thought fit, and not fpare them in any manner; that now they were not in the leaft tired, nor felt the leaft thirft; and that as long as they

fhould

should be commanded by such a king, they could not think themselves mortal men.

Had Alexander always cherished such sentiments as these, he would justly have merited the title of great; but a too glorious an uninterupted series of prosperity, insensibly effaced them from his mind, and made him forget that he was man, contemning the customs of his own country, he laid aside the dress, the manners and way of life of the Macedonian monarchs. In imitation of the Persian kings he turned his palace into a seraglio, filling it with three hundred and sixty concubines, (the same number Darius kept) and with bands of eunuchs, of all mankind the most infamous.

Not satisfied with wearing a Persian robe himself, he also obliged his generals, his friends, and all the grandees of the court, to put on the same dress, which gave them the greatest mortification, not one of them however daring to speak against this innovation, or contradict the prince in any manner.

The veteran soldiers, who had fought under Philip, not having the least idea of sensuality, inveighed publicly against this prodigious luxury, and the numerous vices which the army had learned in Susa and Ecbatana. The soldiers would frequently express themselves in the following terms: " That " they had lost more by victory than they had gain- " ed: but as the Macedonians had thus assumed " the manners and customs of foreigners, they might " properly be said to be conquered. That therefore " all they should reap from their long absence, would " be, to return back into their country in the habit " of Barbarians; that Alexander was ashamed of, " and despised them; that he chose to resemble the

vanquished

" vanquished rather than the victorious; and that
" he, who before had been king of Macedonia, was
" now become one of Darius's lieutenants."

The king was not ignorant of the discontent
which reigned both in his court and army, and endeavoured to recover the esteem and friendship of
both by his beneficence: but slavery, though purchased at ever so high a rate, must necessarily be odious to freeborn men. He therefore thought, that
the safest remedy would be to employ them, and for
that purpose led them against Bessus. But as the
army was encumbered with booty and an useless
train of baggage, that he could scarce move, he first
caused all his own baggage to be carried into a
great square, and afterwards that of his army (such
things excepted as were absolutely necessary) then
ordered the whole to be carried from thence in carts
to a large plain. Every one was in great pain to know
the meaning of all this; but after he had sent away
the horses, he himself set fire to his own things, and
commanded every one to follow his example. Upon
this the Macedonians lighted up the fire with their
own hands, and burnt the rich spoils they had purchased with their blood, and often forced out of the
midst of the flames. Such a sacrifice must certainly
have been made with the utmost reluctance; but the
example the king set them silenced all their complaints, and they seemed less affected at the loss of
their baggage, than at their neglect of military discipline. A short speech the king made, soothed all
their uneasiness; and, being now more able to exert
themselves hereafter, they set out with joy, and marched towards Bactriana. In this march they met with
difficulties which would have quite damped any one

P   but

but Alexander; but nothing could daunt his foul, or check his progress; for he put the strongest confidence in his good fortune, which indeed never forsook that hero, but extricated him from a thousand perils, wherein one would have naturally supposed both himself and his army must have perished.

Being arrived among the Drangæ, a danger to which he had not been accustomed, gave him very great uneasiness; and this was, the report of a conspiracy that was formed against his person. One Dymnus, a man of no figure at court, was the contriver of this treason. He had communicated his execrable design to a young man, Nichomachus by name, who revealed it to Cebalinus his brother. The latter immediately whispered it to Philotas, earnestly entreating him to acquaint the king with it, for the conspirators were to execute their design in three days. Philotas, after applauding his fidelity, waited immediately upon the king and discoursed on a great variety of subjects but without taking the least notice of the plot. This made Cebilanus suspect him, he therefore got another person to disclose it to Alexander. The prince having heard the whole from Cebalinus himself, first commanded Dymnus to be brought before him, who, guessing upon what account he was sent for by the king, ran himself through with his sword, but the guards having prevented this wretch from completing the deed, he was carried to the palace. The king asked him why he thought Philotas more worthy than he was of the kingdom of Macedon? but he was quite speechless; so that, after fetching a deep sigh, he turned his head aside, and breathed his last.

The king afterwards held a council compofed of his chief confidents, likewife the Macedonian foldiers, who affembled under arms, it being a very ancient cuftom for the army, in war time, to take cognizance of capital crimes; and, in times of peace for the people to do fo; fo that the prince had no power on thefe occafions, unlefs a fanction was given to it by the confent of one of thefe bodies; and the king was forced to have recourfe to perfuafion, before he employed his authority.

The refult of this affembly was, that Philotas fhould be put on the rack. The perfons who prefided on that occafion were his moft inveterete enemies, and they made him fuffer every kind of torture. Philotas, at firft difcovered the utmoft refolution and ftrength of mind; the torments he fuffered not being able to force from him a fingle word, not even fo much as a figh. But at laft, conquered by pain, he confeffed himfelf to be guilty, named feveral accomplices, and even accufed his own father. The next day the anfwers of Philotas were read in a full affembly, he himfelf being prefent. Upon the whole, he was unanimoufly fentenced to die; immediately after which he was ftoned, according to the cuftom of Macedonia, with fome others of the confpirators.

The condemnation of Philotas brought on that of Parmenio: whether it were that Alexander really believed him guilty, or was afraid of the father now he had put the fon to death, Polydamus, one of the lords of the court, was appointed to fee the execution performed. He had been one of Parmenio's moft intimate friends, if we may give that name to courtiers, who affect only their own fortunes. This was

was the very reason of his being nominated, because no one could suspect that he was sent with any such orders against Parmenio. He therefore set out for Media, where that general commanded the army, and was entrusted with the king's treasures, which amounted to an hundred and fourscore thousand talents, about twenty-seven millions sterling. Alexander had given him several letters for Cleander the king's lieutenant in the province; and for the principal officers. Two were for Parmenio; one of them from Alexander, and the other sealed with Philotas's seal, as if he had been alive, to prevent the father from harbouring the least suspicion. Polydamus was but eleven days in his journey, and alighted in the night time at Cleander's. After having taken all the precautions necessary, they went together, with a great number of attendants to meet Parmenio, who at this time was walking in a park of his own. The moment Polydamus spied him, though at a great distance, he ran to embrace him with an air of the utmost joy; and after compliments, intermixed with the strongest indications of friendship, had passed on both sides, he gave him Alexander's letter. In the opening it, he asked him what the king was doing; to which Polydamus replied, that he would know by his majesty's letter. Parmenio, after perusing it, said as follows: " The king is pre-
" paring to march against the Arachosii. How glo-
" rious a prince is this, who will not suffer himself to
" take a moment's rest! However, he ought to be
" a little tender of himself, now he has acquired so
" much glory." He afterwards opened the letter which was written in Philotas's name; and, by his countenance, seemed pleased with the contents of it.

At

At that very inftant Cleander thruft a dagger into his fide, then made another thruft in his throat ; and the reft gave him feveral wounds, even after he was dead.

Alexander was fenfible, that fuch cruel executions might alienate the affections of the troops, of which he had a proof, by the letters they fent into Macedonia, which were intercepted by his order ; concluding therefore that it would be proper for him to feparate, from the reft of the army, fuch foldiers as had moft diftinguifhed themfelves by their murmurs and complaints, left their feditious difcourfes fhould fpread the fame fpirit of difcontent, he formed a feparate body of thefe, the command of which he gave to Leonidas ; this kind of ignominy being the only punifhment he inflicted on them. But they were fo ftrongly affected with it, that they endeavoured to wipe out the difgrace it brought upon them, by a bravery, a fidelity, and an obedience, which they obferved ever afterwards.

To prevent the ill confequences that might arife from this fecret difcontent, Alexander fet out upon his march, and continued to purfue Beffus. After a dangerous march he arrived at a mountain called Paropamefus (a part of Caucafus) where his army underwent inexpreffible fatigues, through wearinefs, thirft, cold, and the fnows, which had killed a great number of his foldiers. Beffus laid wafte all the country which lay between him and Mount Caucafus, in order that the want of provifions and forage might deprive Alexander of an opportunity of purfuing him. He indeed fuffered very much, but nothing could check his vigour. After his army had taken fome repofe, he advanced towards Aornos and
P. 2.   Bactra,

Bactra, the two strongest cities of Bactriana, and took them both. At Alexander's approach, about seven or eight thousand Bactrians, who till then had adhered very firmly to Bessus, abandoned him to a man, and each retired to his respective home.

About this time, Spitamenes, who was Bessus's chief confident, formed a conspiracy against him, in concert with two more of his principal officers. Having seized his person, they put him in chains, forced his diadem from his head, tore to pieces the royal robe of Darius he had put on, and set him on horseback, in order to give him up to Alexander.

That prince arrived at a little city inhabited by the Branchidae. These were the descendants of a family who had dwelt in Miletus, and were intrusted with the treasure of the temple called Didymaon, which they treacherously delivered up to Xerxes, who in return settled them in a very flourishing condition in Upper Asia. Alexander left it to the choice of the Milesians who were in his army, of either revenging the injury they had formerly done them, or of pardoning them in consideration of their common extraction. The Milesians being so much divided in opinion, that they could not agree among themselves, Alexander undertook the decision himself. Accordingly the next day he commanded his phalanx to surround the city; and a signal being given, they were ordered to plunder that abode of traitors, and put every one of them to the sword, which inhuman order was executed with the same barbarity as it was given. All the citizens, at the very time that they were going to pay homage to Alexander, were murdered in the streets, and in their houses; no manner of regard being had to their

cries

cries and tears, nor the least distinction made of age or sex. They even pulled up the very foundations of the walls, in order that not the least traces of that city might remain. Such was the total destruction of these ill-fated citizens, for the crimes their fathers had committed upwards of one hundred and fifty years before.

A little after Bessus was brought to Alexander, not only bound but stark naked. Spitamanes held him by a chain, which went round his neck. In presenting him to the king, he said, " I have at last " revenged both you and Darius, my kings and " masters. I bring you a wretch who assassinated " his own sovereign; and who is now treated in the " same manner as himself gave the first example of. " Alas! Why cannot Darius see this spectacle!" Alexander, after having greatly applauded Spitamanes, turned about to Bessus, and spoke thus: " Thou must surely have been inspired with the rage " and fury of a tyger, otherwise thou wouldest not " have dared to load a king, from whom thou hadst " received so many instances of favour, with chains, " and afterwards murder him! Be gone from my " sight, thou monster of cruelty and perfidiousness." The king said no more, but sending for Oxatres, Darius's brother, he gave Bessus to him, in order that he might suffer all the ignominy he deserved; suspending however his execution, that he might be judged in the general assembly of the Persians.

SECT.

SECT. XII. *Alexander after taking a great many cities in Bactriana, builds one near the river Iaxarthe, which he calls by his own name. The Scythians alarmed at the building of this city, send ambassadors to the king. He gains a signal victory over the Scythians. He checks and punishes the insurrection of the Sogdians, sends Bessus to Ecbatana, to be put to death, and takes the city of Petra, which was thought impregnable.*

ALEXANDER, insatiable of victory and conquests, still marched forward in search of new nations whom he might subdue. After recruiting his cavalry, which had suffered very much by their long and dangerous marches, he advanced to the Iaxarthes.

Not far from this river the Barbarians rushing suddenly from their mountains, came and attacked Alexander's forces, and having carried off a great number of prisoners, they retired to their lurking holes, in which were twenty thousand, who fought with bows and slings. The king went and besieged them in person, and being one of the foremost in the attack, he was shot with an arrow in the bone of his leg, and the iron point stuck in the wound. The Macedonians, who were greatly alarmed, carried him off immediately, yet not so secretly but that the Barbarians knew of it. The next day they sent ambassadors to the king, who ordered them to be immediately brought in, when taking off the bandage that covered his wound, he showed them his leg. These assured him, that as soon as they heard of his being wounded, they were as much afflicted as the Macedonians could possibly be, and could they have found the person who shot the arrow, they would have delivered

livered him up to Alexander; that none but impious wretches would wage war againſt the gods; that being vanquiſhed by his unparelleled bravery, they ſubmitted to him. The king, after taking back his priſoners, accepted their homage.

After this he ſet out upon his march, and arrived at Maracanda, the capital of Sogdiana, which he took; and after leaving a conſiderable garriſon there, he burnt and laid waſte all the plains. From thence he proceeded to the river Iaxarthes, where he had marked out a ſpot of ground proper for building a city, in order to curb the nations he had conquered, and thoſe he intended to ſubdue. But this deſign was retarded by the rebellion of the Sogdians, which was followed by the Bactrians. Alexander diſpatched Spitamanes to bring them back to their allegiance; but he himſelf had been chiefly inſtrumental in this inſurrection. The king ſurpriſed at this treachery, was determined to take vengeance of him in the moſt ſignal manner. He then marched to Cyropolis, which he took by ſtorm, and after plundering the city, razed it to the very foundations. From hence he went to Memaceni, no place ever made a more vigorous defence than this; Alexander not only loſt his beſt ſoldiers before it, but was himſelf expoſed to very great danger; a ſtone ſtriking him with ſo much violence on the head, that it deprived him of his ſenſes, the whole army thought him dead; but the inſtant he recovered, without ſtaying till his wound was healed, he puſhed on the ſiege with greater vigour than before, having made a breach in the wall and entered the city, he burnt it to the ground, and put all the inhabitants to the ſword. Several other cities met the ſame fate. This was a third rebellion of the

Sogdians.

Sogdians. Alexander had pardoned them twice before. They loſt above an hundred and twenty thouſand men in theſe different ſieges. The king afterwards ſent Menedemus with three thouſand foot and eight hundred horſe, to Maracanda, whence Spitamenes had drove the Macedonian garriſon, and ſhut himſelf up there.

With regard to himſelf, he returned back and encamped on the Iaxarthes, where he ſurrounded with walls the whole ſpot of ground which his army covered, and built a city on it, containing three leagues in circumference, which he called Alexandria; and to people his new city, he ranſomed all the priſoners he could meet with, ſettled ſuch of his ſoldiers there who were worn out in his ſervice, and permitted many natives of the country, at their own requeſt to inhabit it.

But the king of thoſe Scythians who live on the other ſide of the Iaxarthes, fearing that this city would prove a yoke for them, they ſent a great body of ſoldiers to demoliſh it, and to drive the Macedonians to a greater diſtance. Alexander, who had no deſign of attacking the Scythians, finding them make ſeveral incurſions, even in his ſight, in a very inſolent manner, was much perplexed; eſpecially when advice was brought him at the ſame time, that the body of troops he had ordered to Maracanda, had been all cut to pieces; however he immediately prepared to croſs the river, and in three days time, his ſoldiers completed twelve thouſand rafts or floats for that purpoſe.

As every thing was ready for the march, ſeveral Scythian ambaſſadors arrived to the number of twenty, according to the cuſtom of their country, who all rode

rode through the camp, defiring to fpeak with the king. Alexander having fent for them into his tent, defired them to fet down. They gazed attentively upon him a long time without fpeaking a word, being very probably furprifed, to find that his air and ftature did not anfwer the high idea they had entertained of him from his fame. At length the oldeft of the ambaffadors addreffed Alexander in the following words:

"Had the gods given thee a body proportion-
"able to thy ambition, the whole univerfe would
"have been too little for thee. With one hand
"thou wouldeft touch the eaft, and with the other
"the weft; and not fatisfied with this, thou would-
"eft follow the fun, and know where he hides him-
"felf. Such as thou art, thou yet afpireft after what
"it will be impoffible for thee to attain. Thou
"croffeft over from Europe into Afia; and when
"thou fhalt have fubdued all the race of men, then
"thou wilt make war againft rivers, forefts and wild
"beafts. Doft thou not know, that tall trees are
"many years a growing, but may be torn up in an
"hour's time; that the lion ferves fometimes for
"food to the fmalleft birds; that iron, though fo
"very hard, is confumed by ruft; in a word, that
"there is nothing fo ftrong which may not be def-
"troyed by the weakeft thing?

"What have we to do with thee? We never fet
"foot in thy country. May not thofe who inhabit
"woods, be allowed to live without knowing who
"thou art, and whence thou comeft? We will neith-
"er command over, or fubmit to any man. And
"that thou mayeft be fenfible what kind of people
"the Scythians are, know, that we received from
heaven,

" heaven, as a rich prefent, a yoke of oxen, a plough-
" fhare, a dart, a javelin, and a cup. Thefe we make
" ufe of, both with our friends, and againft our ene-
" mies. To our friends we give corn, which we
" procure by the labour of our oxen ; with them we
" offer wine to the gods in our cup ; and with re-
" gard to our enemies, we combat them at a dif-
" tance with our arrows, and near at hand with our
" javelins. It is with thefe we formerly conquered
" the moft warlike nations, fubdued the moft power-
" ful kings, laid wafte all Afia, and opened ourfelves
" a way into the heart of Egypt.

" But thou, who boafteft thy coming to extirpate
" robbers, thou thyfelf art the greateft robber upon
" earth. Thou haft plundered all nations thou
" overcameft. Thou haft poffeffed thyfelf of Lydia,
" invaded Syria, Perfia, and Bactriana ; thou art
" forming a defign to march as far as India, and
" thou now comeft hither to feize upon our herds of
" cattle. The great poffeffions thou haft, only make
" thee covet more eagerly what thou haft not. Doft
" thou not fee how long the Bactrians have checked
" thy progrefs ? Whilft thou art fubduing thefe, the
" Sogdians revolt, and victory is to thee only the
" occafion of war.

" Pafs but the Iaxarthes, and thou wilt behold
" the great extent of our plains. It will be in vain
" for thee to purfue the Scythians : and I defy thee
" ever to overtake them. Our poverty will be more
" active than thy army, laden with the fpoils of fo
" many nations ; and, when thou fhalt fancy us at a
" great diftance, thou wilt fee us rufh fuddenly on
" thy camp ; for we purfue, and fly from our ene-
" mies, with equal fpeed. I am informed that the

" Greeks

" Greeks speak jestingly of the Scythian solitudes;
" and that they are even become a proverb; but we
" are fonder of our deserts, than of thy great cities
" and fruitful plains. Let me observe to thee, that
" fortune is slippery; hold her fast therefore, for
" fear she should escape thee. Put a curb to thy fe-
" licity, if thou desirest to continue in possession of it.

" If thou art a god, thou oughtest to do good to
" mortals, and not deprive them of their possessions:
" if thou art a mere man, reflect always on what thou
" art. They whom thou shalt not molest, will be
" thy true friends; the strongest friendships being
" contracted between equals; and they are esteem-
" ed equals, who have not tried their strength against
" each other: but do not imagine, that those whom
" thou conquerest can love thee; for there is no
" such thing as friendship between a master and his
" slave, and a forced peace is soon followed by a war.

" To conclude, do not fancy that the Scythians
" will take an oath in their concluding an alliance.
" The only oath among them, is to keep their word
" without swearing. Such cautions as these do in-
" deed become Greeks, who sign their treaties, and
" call upon the gods to witness them; but, with re-
" gard to us, our religion consists in being sincere,
" and in keeping the promises we have made. That
" man who is not ashamed to break his word with
" men, is not ashamed of deceiving the gods; and
" of what use could friends be to thee whom thou
" couldest not trust? Consider that we will guard
" both Europe and Asia for thee. We extend
" as far as Thrace, and we are told, that this
" country is contiguous to Macedonia. The river
" Iaxarthes only divides us from Bactriana. Thus

" we

" we are thy neighbours on both sides. Consider,
" therefore, whether thou wilt have us for friends, or
" enemies."

The Barbarian spoke thus: to whom the king
made but a very short answer; "That he would take
" advantage both of his own good fortune, and of
" their counsel; of his good fortune, by still con-
" tinuing to rely upon it; and of their counsel, by
" not attempting any thing rashly." Having dismissed the ambassadors, his army embarked on the
rafts which by this time were got ready.

The army found great difficulty in crossing the
river. Every thing conspired to intimidate them;
the clamour and confusion, that are inseparable from
such an enterprize; the rapidity of the stream; and
the sight of a numerous army drawn up in battle-
array on the opposite shore. However, the presence
of Alexander, who was ever the foremost in encoun-
tering dangers, made them neglect their own safety,
and be concerned for his only. As soon as the Macedonians began to draw near the shore, they who
carried shields rose up together, when throwing their
javelins with a strong arm, every weapon did execution. When they perceived that the enemy, overpowered with that shower of shafts, began to retire,
and draw their horses back, they leaped on the shore
with incredible swiftness, and, animating one another, began the charge with vigour. In this disorder, the troopers, whose horses were ready bridled,
rushed upon the enemy, and quite broke them.

Nothing was heard in the Macedonian army, but
shouts of joy and victory, whilst they continued to
attack the Barbarians with the utmost fury: The
latter not being able to stand so fierce an onset, fled as
fast

fast as their horses would carry them; for these were the cavalry only. The Macedonians pursued them beyond the boundaries or limits of Bacchus, which were marked out by great stones ranged pretty close to one another, and by great trees, the trunks of which were covered with ivy. The heat of the pursuit carried them so far that they did not return back into their camp, till after midnight; having killed a great number of the enemy, and taken many more prisoners, with eighteen hundred horses. On Alexander's side there were but sixty troopers slain, and about one hundred foot, with a thousand wounded. Alexander sent back all their prisoners without ransom, to show, that not animosity, but a thirst of glory, had prompted him to make war against so valiant a nation.

The report of this victory, and much more the clemency with which the king treated the vanquished, greatly increased his reputation. The Scythians had always been considered as invincible; but after their defeat it was owned that every nation in the world ought to yield to the Macedonians. The Sacæ, who were a powerful nation, sent an embassy to Alexander, by which they submitted themselves to him, and requested his friendship. The Scythians themselves made an apology, and declared they were ready to obey the command of the victorious prince.

Alexander being so happily free from the care and trouble of this important war, bent his whole thoughts on Maracanda, in which the traitor Spitamanes had fortified himself. At the first news of Alexander's approach, he had fled away, and withdrawn into Bactriana. The king not caring to pursue him thither, returned back and sacked Sogdiana.

Among

Among the Sogdians that were taken prisoners, there were thirty young men, who were the greatest lords of the country. These being told that they were led to execution by Alexander's command, began to sing songs of joy, to leap and dance, discovering all the indications of an immoderate joy. The king, surprised to see them go to death with so much gaiety, had them brought before him; when he asked them, how they came to break into such transports of joy, when they saw death before their eyes? they answered, that they should have been afflicted, had any other person but himself put them to death; but as they would be restored to their ancestors by the command of so great a monarch, who had vanquished all nations. Alexander, admiring their magnanimity, asked whether they would desire to be pardoned, upon condition that they should no longer be his enemies? they answered, he might be assured they had never been his enemies; but that, as he had attacked them, they had defended themselves. The king asked them further, what pledges they would give him of their sincerity? "No other (answered "they) but the same life we receive from your good- "ness, and which we shall be always ready to give "back, whenever you shall require it." They proved as good as their word. Four of them, whom he took into his body guards, endeavoured to rival the Macedonians in zeal and fidelity.

The king, after having left a small number of forces in Sogdiana, marched to Bactria, where, having assembled all his generals, he commanded Bessus to be brought before them; when, after reproaching him for his treachery, he caused his nose and ears to be cut off, and then sent him to Ecbatana, there

there to suffer whatever punishment Darius's mother should think proper to inflict upon him. Plutarch has left us an account of this execution. Four trees were bent, by main force towards each other; and to each of these trees one of the limbs of this traitor's body was fastened. Afterwards these trees being let return to their natural position, they flew back with so much violence, that each tore away the limb which was fixed to it.

Alexander received at this time, both from Macedonia and Greece, a large number of recruits, amounting to upwards of sixteen thousand men. By this reinforcement, he was enabled to subdue all those who had rebelled, and to curb them for the future.

(b) All things were now restored to a profound tranquility. There remained but one strong hold, called the rock of Oxus, which was defended by Arimazes with thirty thousand soldiers under his command. This rock which was very high and craggy on all sides, was accessable only by a single path that was cut in it. The king, after viewing its works was in suspence whether he should besiege it, but as it was his character to aim at the marvellous in all things, and to attempt impossibilities, he resolved to try if he could not overcome, on this occasion, nature itself, which seemed to have fortified this rock in such a manner as had rendered it absolutely impregnable. However, before he formed the siege, he summoned those Barbarians, but in mild terms, to submit to him. Arimazes received this offer in a very haughty manner; and after using several insulting expressions, asked, " Whether

Q 2 Alexander,

(*) *A. M.* 3676; *Ant. J. C.* 328.

" Alexander, who was able to do all things, could
" fly alſo'; and whether nature had, on a ſudden,
" given him wings ?"

Alexander was highly exaſperated at this anſwer. He therefore gave orders for ſelecting, from among the mountaineers who were in his army, three hundred of the moſt active and dextrous. Theſe being brought to him, he addreſſed them thus : " It was
" in your company, brave young men, that I ſtorm-
" ed ſuch places as were thought impregnable ;
" that I made my way over mountains covered with
" eternal ſnows ; croſſed rivers, and broke through
" the paſſes of Silicia. This rock, which you ſee,
" has but one outlet, which alone is defended by the
" Barbarians, who neglect every other part. There
" is no watch or centinel, except on that ſide which
" faces our camp. If you ſearch very narrowly, you
" certainly will meet with ſome path that leads to
" the top of the rock. Nothing has been made ſo
" inacceſſible by nature, as not to be ſurmounted by
" valour ; and it was only by our attempting, what
" no one before had hopes of effecting, that we poſ-
" ſeſſed ourſelves of Aſia. Get up to the ſummit,
" and when you ſhall have made yourſelves maſters
" of it, ſet up a white ſtandard there as a ſignal ;
" and be aſſured, that I then will certainly diſen-
" gage you from the enemy, and draw them upon
" myſelf, by making a diverſion." At the ſame time that the king gave out this order, he made them the moſt noble promiſes ; but the pleaſing him, was conſidered by them as the greateſt of all rewards. Fired therefore with the moſt noble ardour, and fancying they had already reached the ſummit, they ſet out, after having provided themſelves with wedges

to drive into the stones, cramp-irons, and thick ropes.

The king went round the mountain with them, and commanded them to begin their march * at the second watch of the night, by that part which should seem to them of easiest access; beseeching the gods to guide their steps. They then took provisions for two days; and being armed with swords and javelins only, they began to ascend the mountain, walking sometime on foot; afterwards, when it was necessary for them to climb, some forced their wedges into the stones which projected forwards, and by that means raised themselves; others thrust their cramp-irons into the stones that were frozen, to keep themselves from falling in so slippery a way; in fine, others driving in their wedges with great strength, made them serve as so many scaling ladders. They spent the whole day in this manner, hanging against the rock, and exposed to numerous dangers and difficulties, being obliged to struggle at the same time with snow, cold, and wind. Nevertheless, the hardest task was yet to come; and the farther they advanced, the higher the rock seemed to rise. But that which terrified them most, was the sad spectacle of some of their comrades falling down precipices, whose unhappy fate was a warning to them of what they themselves might expect. Notwithstanding this, they still advanced forward, and exerted themselves so vigorously, that, in spite of all these difficulties, they at last got to the top of the rock. They then were all inexpressible weary, and many of them had even lost the use of some of their limbs. Night and drowsiness came upon them at the same time, so that

* about ten o'clock.

that, difperfing themfelves in fuch diftant parts of the rock as were free from fnows, they laid down in them, and flept till day-break. At laft waking from a deep fleep, and looking on all fides to difcover the place where fo many people could lie hid, they faw fmoke below them, which fhowed them the haunt of the enemy. They then put up the fignal, as had been agreed; and their whole company drawing up, thirty-two were found wanting, who had loft their lives in the afcent.

In the mean time the king, equally fired with a defire of ftorming the fortreffes, and ftruck with the vifible dangers to which thofe men were expofed, continued on foot the whole day, gazing upon the rock, and he himfelf did not retire to reft till dark. The next morning, by peep of day, he was the firft who perceived the fignal. Neverthelefs he was ftill in doubt whether he might truft his eyes, becaufe of the falfe fplendour which breaks out at day-break; but the light increafing, he was fure of what he faw. Sending therefore for Cophes, who before, by his command, had furrounded the Barbarians, he difpatched him a fecond time, with an exhortation to think better of the matter; and in cafe they fhould ftill depend upon the ftrength of the place, he then was ordered to fhow them the band of men behind their backs, who were got to the fummit of the rock. Cophes employed all the arguments poffible, to engage Arimazes to capitulate; reprefenting to him, that he would gain the king's favour, in cafe he did not interrupt the great defigns he meditated, by obliging him to make fome ftay before that rock. Animazes fent a haughtier and more infolent anfwer than before, and commanded him

him to retire. Then Cophes taking him by the hand, defired he would come out of the cave with him, which the Barbarian doing, he fhowed him the Macedonians pofted over his head, and faid in an infulting tone of voice, You fee that Alexander's foldiers have wings. In the mean time, the trumpets were heard to found in every part of the Macedonian camp, and the whole army fhouted aloud, and cried victory! Thefe things, though of little confequence in themfelves, did neverthelefs, as often happens, throw the Barbarians into fo great a confternation, that without once reflecting how few were got to the fummit, they thought themfelves loft. Upon this, Cophes was recalled, and thirty of the chief among the Barbarians were fent back with him, who agreed to furrender up the place, upon condition that their lives might be fpared. The king, notwithftanding the ftrong oppofition he might meet with, was fo exafperated at the haughtinefs of Arimazes, that he refufed to grant them any terms of capitulation. Arimazes, however was fo blinded by fear, and concluding himfelf abfolutely loft, came down, with his relations and the principal nobility of the country, into Alexander's camp. But this prince, who was not mafter of his anger, forgetting what the faith of treaty and humanity required on this occafion, caufed them all to be fcourged with rods, and afterwards to be fixed to croffes, at the foot of the fame rock. The multitudes of people who furrendered, with all the booty, were given to the inhabitants of the cities which had been newly founded in thofe parts; and Artabazus was left governor of the rock, and the whole province round it.

SECT.

SECT. XIII. *The death of Clitus. Several expeditions of Alexander. He commands worship to be paid to himself, after the manner of the Persians. Discontents arise among the Macedonians. Death of Calisthenes the philosopher.*

ALEXANDER having subdued the Massagetæ and Dahæ, entered Bazaria. In this province are a great number of large parks stocked with deer. Here the king took the diversion of hunting, in which he was exposed to very great peril; for a lion of an enormous size advanced directly to him, but he killed him with a single thrust. Although Alexander came off victorious on this occasion, yet the Macedonians, alarmed at the danger he had run, and the whole army in his person, gave orders, pursuant to the custom of their country, that the king should go no more a hunting on foot, without being attended by some of his courtiers and officers. They were sensible, that a king is not born for his own sake, but for that of his subjects; that he ought to be careful of his own person for their sakes, and reserve his courage for other dangers; and that the being famous for killing beasts (a reputation unworthy of a great prince) ought not to be purchased so dear.

From hence he advanced to Maracanda, where he quelled some tumults which had broke out in that country. Artabazus requesting to be discharged from the government of that province, by reason of his great age, he appointed Clitus his successor. He was an old officer, who had fought under Philip, and signalized himself on many occasions. At the battle of the Granicus, as Alexander was fighting bareheaded, and Rosases had his arm raised, in order to
strike

strike him behind, he covered the king with his shield, and cut off the Barbarian's hand. Hellanice his sister, had nursed Alexander; and he loved her with as much tenderness as if she had been his own mother. As the king from these several considerations had very great respect for Clitus, he entrusted him with the government of one of the most important provinces of his empire, and ordered him to set out the next day.

Before his departure, Clitus was invited in the evening to an entertainment, in which the king, after drinking immoderately, began to celebrate his own exploits; and was so excessively lavish of self-commendation, that he even shocked those very persons who knew that he spoke truth. However, the oldest men in the company held their peace, till beginning to depreciate the warlike acts of Philip, he boasted,
" That the famous victory of Chæronea was won by
" his means; and that the glory of so immortal a
" battle had been torn from him by the malice and
" jealousy of his father. That in the * insurrection
" which broke out between the Macedonians and
" mercenary Greeks, Philip, fainting away after the
" wounds he had received in that tumult, had laid
" himself on the ground; and could not think of a
" better method to save himself, than by lying along
" as dead; that on this occasion, he had covered
" him with his shield, and killed with his own hands
" those who attempted to fall upon him; but that
" his father could not prevail upon himself to con-
" fess this circumstance ingenuously, being vexed
" that he owed his life to his own son. That in the
" war against the Illyrians, he was the only person
                                                    " who

* *This sedition is not mentioned in any other place.*

" who had done any thing, Philip having had no
" manner of fhare in it; and hearing of the defeat
" of the enemy, no otherwife than by the letters he
" fent him. That the perfons worthy of praife were
" not fuch as initiated themfelves in the † myfteries
" of the Samothracians, when they ought to have
" laid wafte all Afia with fire and fword, but thofe
" who had atchieved fuch mighty exploits as fur-
" paffed all belief."

Thefe and the like difcourfes were very pleafing
to the young men, but were fhocking to thofe
advanced in years; efpecially for Philip's fake, under whom they had fought many years. Clitus, who
alfo was intoxicated, turning about to thofe who fat
below him at table, quoted to them a paffage from
‡ Euripides, but in fuch a manner that the king
could only hear his voice, and not the words dif-
tinctly. The fenfe of this paffage was, " That the
" Greeks had done very wrong in ordaining, that
" in the infcriptions engraved on trophies, the names
" of kings only fhould be mentioned; becaufe, by
" thefe means, brave men were robbed of the glory
" they had purchafed with their blood." The king,
fufpecting Clitus had let drop fome difobliging expreffions, afked thofe who fat neareft him, what he
had faid? As no one anfwered, Clitus, raifing his
voice by degrees, began to relate the actions of Philip, and his wars in Greece, preferring them to whatever was doing at that time; which created a great
difpute between the young and old men. Though
the

† *It was ufual for generals, before they fet out on their expeditions, to caufe themfelves to be initiated in thefe myfteries, and offer
facrifices to the gods who prefided in them. Poffibly Philip, by obferving this ceremony, had delayed fome enterprife.*

‡ *In his Andromache.*

the king was prodigiously vexed in his mind, he nevertheless stifled his resentment, and seemed to listen very patiently to all Clitus spoke to his prejudice. It is probable he would have quite suppressed his passion, had Clitus stopped there; but the latter growing more and more insolent, as if determined to exasperate and insult the king, went such lengths, as to defend Parmenio publickly; and to assert, that the destroying of Thebes was but trifling, in comparison of the victory which Philip had gained over the Athenians; and that the old Macedonians, though sometimes unsuccesful, were greatly superior to those who were so rash as to despise them.

Alexander telling him, that in giving cowardice the name of ill success, he was pleading his own cause; Clitus rises up, with his eyes sparkling with wine and anger; "It is nevertheless this hand (said "he to him, extending it at the same time) that sa-"ved your life at the battle of the Granicus. It is "the blood and wounds of these very Macedonians, "who are accused of cowardice, that raised you to "this grandeur. But the tragical end of Parmenio "shows, what reward they and myself may expect "for all our services." This last reproach stung Alexander: However, he still restrained his passion, and only commanded him to leave the table. "He is in the right (says Clytus, as he rose up) not "to bear free born men at his table, who can only "tell him truth. He will do well to pass his life "among Barbarians and slaves, who will be proud "to pay their adoration to his Persian girdle and his "white robe." But now the king, no longer able to suppress his rage, snatched a javelin from one of his guards, and would have killed Clitus on the spot,

spot, had not the courtiers withheld his arm, and Clitus been forced, but with great difficulty, out of the hall. However, he returned into it that moment by another door, singing, with an air of insolence, verses reflecting highly on the prince, who seeing the general near him, struck him with his javelin, and laid him dead at his feet, crying out at the same time, "Go now to Philip, to Parmenio, and to "Attalus."

The king's anger being in a manner extinguished on a sudden in the blood of Clitus, his crime displayed itself to him in its blackest and most dreadful light. He had murdered a man, who indeed abused his patience, but then he had always served him with the utmost zeal and fidelity, and saved his life, though he was ashamed to own it. He had that instant performed the vile office of an executioner, in punishing, by an horrid murder, the uttering of some indiscreet words, which might be imputed to the fumes of wine. With what face could he appear before the sister of Clitus, his nurse, and offer her a hand imbrued in her brother's blood? Upon this he threw himself on his friend's body, forced out the javelin, and would have dispatched himself with it, had not the guards, who rushed in upon him, laid hold of his hands, and forcibly carried him into his own apartment.

He passed that night and the next day in tears. After that groans and lamentations had quite wasted his spirits, he continued speechless, stretched on the ground, and only venting deep sighs. But his friends, fearing his silence would be fatal, forced themselves into his chamber. The king took very little notice of the words that were employed to comfort

fort him; but Ariſtander the ſoothſayer, putting him in mind of a dream, in which he had imagined he ſaw Clitus, cloathed in a black robe, and ſeated at table; and declaring, that all which had then happened, was appointed by the eternal decree of fate, Alexander appeared a little eaſier in his mind. He next was addreſſed by two philoſophers, Caliſthenes and Anaxarchus. The former went up to him with an air of humanity and tenderneſs, and endeavoured to ſuppreſs his grief, by agreeably inſinuating himſelf, and endeavoured to make him recall his reaſon, by reflections of a ſolid nature, drawn from the very eſſence of philoſophy, and by carefully ſhunning all ſuch expreſſions as might renew his affliction, and fret a wound, which, as it was ſtill bleeding, required to be touched with the gentleſt hand. But Anaxarchus did not obſerve this decorum; for the moment he entered, he cried aloud, "How! is this "Alexander, on whom the eyes of the whole world "are fixed? Behold him here extended on the floor, "ſhedding floods of tears, like the meaneſt ſlave! "Does not he know, that he himſelf is a ſupreme "law to his ſubjects; that he conquered merely to "raiſe himſelf to the exalted dignity of a lord and "ſovereign, and not to ſubject himſelf to a vain "opinion?" The king was determined to ſtarve himſelf; ſo that it was with the utmoſt difficulty that his friends prevailed with him to take a little ſuſtenance. The Macedonians declared by a decree, that Clitus had been very juſtly killed; to which decree Anaxarchus the philoſopher had given occaſion, by aſſerting, that the will of princes is the ſupreme law of the ſtate. Alas! how weak are all ſuch reflections againſt the cries of a juſtly alarmed
conſcience,

conscience, which can never be quieted, either by flattery or false arguments!

Alexander, after continuing ten days in Maracanda, in order to recover his spirits, marched into Xenippa, a province bordering upon Scythia,; whither some rebels were retired, all whom he subjected, and gave them a free pardon. From thence he set forward with his army towards the rock Chorienfis, of which Sysimethres was governor. All access to it seemed absolutely impracticable; nevertheless, he at last got near it, after having passed through numberless difficulties; and, by the mediation of of Oxartes, a prince of that country who had adhered to Alexander, he prevailed with Sysimethres to surrender. The king after this left him the government of that place, and promised him very great advantages in case he continued faithful.

Alexander had resolved to attack the Dahæ, because Spitamenes, the chief of the rebels, was among them; but the felicity which always attended him, spared him that labour. The wife of this Barbarian, being no longer able to bear the vagabond, wretched life her husband had forced her to lead, and having often intreated him, but in vain, to surrender himself to the conqueror, she herself murthered him in the night; and, quite covered with his blood, went and carried his head to the king. Alexander was shocked at so horrid a spectacle, and ordered her to be driven ignominiously from the camp.

Alexander, after having drawn his army out of the garrisons, where they had wintered three months, marched towards a country called Gabaza. In his way he met with a dreadful storm of rain, mixed with hail, and so extreme was the cold in this country,

try, that it froze the rain as soon as it fell. The sufferings of the army on this occasion were insupportable. The king, who was the only person invincible to these calamities, rode up and down among the soldiers; comforted and animated them; and pointing at smoke which issued from some distant huts, intreated them to march to them with all the speed possible. Having given orders for the felling of a great number of trees, and laying them in heaps up and down, he had fires made in different places, and by this means saved the army, but upwards of a thousand men lost their lives. The king made up to the officers and soldiers the several losses they had sustained during this fatal storm.

When they were recovered so well as to be able to march, he went into the country of the Sacæ, which he soon over-run and laid waste. Soon after this, Oxarthes received him in his palace, and invited him to a sumptuous banquet, in which he displayed all the magnificence of the Barbarians. He had a daughter, called Roxana, a young lady whose exquisite beauty was heightened by all the charms of wit and good sense. Alexander found her charms irresistable, and made her his wife; covering his passion with the specious pretence of uniting the two nations, in such bands as should improve their mutual harmony, by blending their interests, and throwing down all distinctions between the conquerors and the conquered. This marriage displeased the Macedonians very much, and exasperated his chief courtiers, to see him make one of his slaves his father in-law: but as, after his murdering Clitus, no one dared to speak to him with freedom, they applauded what he did with their eyes and countenances, which can adapt themselves wonderfully to flattery and servile complacency.

In fine; having resolved to march into India, and embark from thence on the ocean, he commanded (in order that nothing might be left behind to check his designs) that thirty thousand young men should be brought him, all completely armed, out of the several provinces, to serve him at the same time as hostages and soldiers. In the mean while, he sent Craterus against some of the rebels, whom he easily defeated.

All things being ready for their setting out, he thought proper to reveal the design he had so long meditated, viz. to have divine honours paid him; and was solely intent on the means for putting that design in execution. He was resolved, not only to be called, but to be believed, the son of Jupiter. He therefore appointed a festival, and made an incredibly pompous banquet, to which he invited the greatest lords of his court, both Macedonians, and Greeks, and most of the highest quality among the Persians. With these he sat down at table for some time, after which he withdrew. Upon this, Cleon, one of his flatterers, began to speak, and expatiated very much on the praises of the king, as had before been agreed upon. He made a long detail of the high obligations they had to him, all which (he observed) they might acknowledge and repay at a very easy expence, merely with two grains of incense, which they should offer him as to a god, without the least scruple, since they believed him such. To this purpose he cited the example of the Persians. He took notice, that Hercules himself, and Bacchus, were not ranked among the deities, till will after they had surmounted the envy of their cotemporaries. That in case the rest should not care to pay this justice to Alexander's merit, he himself was resolved to show them the way, and to worship him if he should come into the hall. But that all of them must do their duty, especially those that professed wisdom, who ought to serve to the rest as an example of the veneration due to so great a monarch.

It appeared plainly that this speech was directed to Callisthenes. He was related to Aristotle, who had presented him to Alexander his pupil, that he might attend upon that monarch in the war of Persia. He was considered, upon account of his wisdom and gravity, as the fittest person to give him such counsel, as was most capable of preserving him from those excesses, into which his youth and fiery temper might hurry him: but he was accused of not possessing the gentle, insinuating behaviour of courts; and of not knowing a certain medium, between grovelling complacency, and inflexible obstinacy. Aristotle had attempted, but to no purpose, to soften the severity of his temper; and foreseeing the ill consequences, with which his disagreeable liberty of speaking his mind might be attended, he used often to repeat the following verse of Homer to him;

"*My son thy freedom will abridge thy days.*"

And his prediction was but too true. This philosopher, seeing that every one, on this occasion, continued in deep silence, and that the eyes of the whole assembly were fixed on him, made a speech, which was doubtless just enough. However, it often happens, when a subject is bound in duty to oppose the inclinations of his sovereign, that the most cautious and most respectful zeal is considered as insolence.

lence and rebellion. "Had the king (said he) been
" present when thou madest thy speech, none among
" us would then have attempted to answer thee, for
" he himself would have interrupted thee, and not
" have suffered thee to prompt him to assume the
" customs of Barbarians, in casting an odium on his
" person and glory, by so servile an adulation, but
" since he is absent, I will answer thee in his name.
" I consider Alexander as worthy of all the honours
" that can be paid a mortal; but there is a difference
" between the worship of the gods and that of men.
" The former includes temples, altars, prayers, and
" sacrifices; the latter is confined to praises only,
" and awful respect. We salute the latter, and look
" upon it as glorious to pay them submission, obe-
" dience, and fidelity ; but we adore the former, we
" institute festivals to their honour, and sing hymns
" and spiritual songs to their glory. The worship
" of the gods does itself vary, according to their
" rank; and the homage we pay to Castor and Pol-
" lux, is not like that with which we adore Mercury
" and Jupiter. We must not therefore confound
" all things, either by bringing down the gods to the
" condition of mortals, or by raising a mortal to the
" state of a god. Alexander would be justly offend-
" ed should we pay to another person the homage
" due to his sacred person only ; ought we not to
" dread the indignation of the gods as much, should
" we bestow upon mortals, the honours due to them.
" alone ? I am sensible that our monarch is vastly,
" superior, to the rest ; he is the greatest of kings,
" and the most glorious of all conquerors ; but then
" he is a man, not a god. To obtain this title, he
" must first be divested of his mortal frame ; but
                                          " this

" this is greatly our intereſt to wiſh may not happen,
" but as late as poſſible. The Greeks did not wor-
" ſhip Hercules till after his death; and that not
" till the oracle had expreſsly commanded it. The
" Perſians are cited as an example for our imitation;
" but how long is it that the vanquiſhed have given
" law to the victor? Can we forget that Alexander
" croſſed the Hellefpont, not to ſubject Greece to
" Aſia, but Aſia to Greece !"

The deep ſilence which all the company obſerved whilſt Calliſthenes ſpoke, was an indication, in ſome meaſure, of their thoughts. The king who ſtood behind the tapeſtry all the time, heard whatever had paſſed. He thereupon ordered Cleon to be told, That without infiſting any farther, he would only require the Perſians to fall proſtrate, according to their uſual cuſtom; a little after which he came in, pretended he had been buſied in ſome affair of importance. Immediately the Perſians fell proſtrate to adore him. Polyſperchon, who ſtood near him, obſerving that one of them bowed ſo low that his chin touched the ground, bid him, in a rallying tone of voice to ſtrike harder. The king, offended at this joke, threw Polyſperchon into priſon, and broke up the aſſembly. However he afterwards pardoned him, but Calliſthenes was not ſo fortunate.

To rid himſelf of him, he laid to his charge a crime of which he was no ways guilty. Hermolaus, one of the young officers who attended upon the king in all places, had, upon account of ſome private pique, formed a conſpiracy againſt him; but it was very happily diſcovered, the inſtant it was to be put in execution. The criminals were ſeized, put to the torture, and executed. Not one among them had
accuſed

accused Callisthenes; but having been very intimate with Hermolaus, that alone was sufficient. Accordingly he was thrown into a dungeon, loaded with irons, and the most grievous torments were inflicted on him, in order to extort a confession of guilt. But he insisted upon his innocence to the last, and expired in the midst of his tortures.

Alexander, by this dreadful example, deprived all virtuous men of the opportunity of exhorting him to those things which were for his true interest. From that instant no one spoke with freedom in the council; even those, who had the greatest love for the public good, and a personal affection for Alexander, thought themselves not obliged to undeceive him. After this, nothing was listened to but flattery, which gained such an ascendant over that prince, as entirely depraved him, and justly punished him, for having sacrificed, to the wild ambition of having adoration paid him, the most virtuous man about his person.

SECT. XIV. *Alexander sets out for India. He besieges and takes several cities which appeared impregnable, and is often in danger of his life. He crosses the river Indus, afterwards the Hydaspes, and gains a signal victory over Porus, whom he restores to his throne.*

ALEXANDER, to stop the murmurs and discontents which arose among his soldiers, sets out for India. He had read in the ancient fables of Greece, that Bacchus and Hercules, both sons of Jupiter, as himself was, had marched so far. He was determined

ned not to be surpassed by them: and there were not wanting flatterers, who applauded this wild, chimerical design. Alexander having entered India, all the petty kings of these countries came to meet him, and make their submission. They declared that he was the third son of Jupiter, who had arrived in their country: that they had known Bacchus and Hercules no otherwise than by fame; but as for Alexander, they had the happiness to see him, and to enjoy his presence. The king received them with the utmost humanity, commanding them to accompany him, and serve him as guides. As no more of them came in to pay their homage, he detached Hephæstion and Perdicas with part of his forces, commanding them to subdue all who should refuse to submit. But finding he was obliged to cross several rivers, he caused boats to be built in such a form, that they could be taken to pieces; the several parts of them to be carried upon waggons, and afterwards put together again. Then, having commanded Craterus to follow him with his phalanx, he himself marched before, with his cavalry and light armed troops; and, after a slight engagement, he defeated those who had dared to make head against him, and pursued them to the next city, into which they fled. Craterus being come up, the king, in order to terrify, on a sudden, those nations who had not yet felt the power of the Macedonian arms, commanded his soldiers to burn down the fortifications of that place, which he besieged in a regular way, and to put all the inhabitants of it to the sword. But as he was going round the walls on horseback, he was wounded by an arrow. Notwithstanding this accident, he took the city, after which he

made

made dreadful havock of all the soldiers and inhabitants, and did not so much as spare the houses.

After subduing this nation, which was of great consequence, he marched towards the city of Nysa, and encamped pretty near its walls, behind a forest that hid it. The besieged having attempted a sally with ill success, a faction arose in the city, some being of opinion, that it would be best for them to surrender, whilst others were for holding out the siege. This coming to the king's ear, he only blocked up the city, and did not do the inhabitants any further injury; till at last tired out with the length of the siege, they surrendered at discretion.

He marched from thence to a country called Dædala, which had been abandoned by the inhabitants, who had fled for shelter to inaccessible mountains, as also those of Acedera, into which he afterwards entered. This obliged him to change his method of war, and to disperse his forces in different places, by which means the enemy were all defeated at once: no resistance was made any where, and those who were so courageous as to wait the coming up of the Macedonians, were all cut to pieces. Ptolemy took several little cities the instant he sat down before them: Alexander carried the large ones, and, after uniting all his forces, passed the river * Choaspes, and left Cœnus to besiege a rich and populous city, called Bazica by the inhabitants.

He afterwards marched towards Magosa, whose king, called Assacanus, was lately dead, and Cleophes, his mother, ruled the province and city. There were thirty thousand foot in it, and both nature and art seemed to have united their endeavours

in

---

* *This is not the Choaspes which runs by Susa.*

in raising its fortifications; for towards the east, it is surrounded with a very rapid river, the banks of which are steep, and difficult of access; and on the west are high craggy rocks, at the foot whereof are caves, which, through length of time, had increased into a kind of abysses; and where these fail, a trench, of an astonishing height, is raised with incredible labour.

Whilst Alexander was going round the city, to view its fortifications, he was shot with an arrow in the calf of his leg; but he only pulled out the weapon; and, without so much as binding up the wound, mounted his horse, and continued to view the outward fortifications of the city. But as he rode with his leg downwards, and the congealing of the blood put him to great pain, it is related that he cried, "Every one swears that I am the son of "Jupiter, but my wound makes me sensible that "I am a man." However, he did not leave the place till he had seen every thing; and given all the necessary orders. Some of the soldiers, therefore, demolished such houses as stood without the city, and with the rubbish of them they filled up the gulphs above mentioned. Others threw great trunks of trees and huge stones into them; and all laboured with so much vigour, that in nine days the works were completed, and the towers were raised upon them.

The king, without waiting till his wound was healed, visited the works, and after applauding the soldiers for their great dispatch, he caused the engines to be brought forward, whence a great number of darts were discharged against those who defended the walls. But that which most terrified the Barbarians,

Barbarians, was thofe towers of a vaft height, which feemed to them to move of themfelves. This made them imagine, that they were made to advance by the gods, and that thofe battering rams which beat down walls, and the javelins thrown by engines, the like of which they had never feen, could not be the effect of human ftrength; fo that, perfuaded that it would be impoffible for them to defend the city, they withdrew into the citadel; but not finding themfelves more fecure there, they fent ambaffadors to propofe a furrender. The queen afterwards came and met Alexander, attended by a great number of ladies, who all brought him wine in cups, by way of facrifice. The king gave her a very gracious reception, and reftored her to her kingdom.

From hence Polyfpherchon was fent with an army to befiege the city of Ora, which he foon took. Moft of its inhabitants had withdrawn to the rock called Arnos. There was a tradition, that Hercules having befieged this rock, an earthquake had forced him to quit the fiege. There are not on this rock, as on many others, gentle declivities of eafy accefs; but it rifes like a bank; and being very wide at the bottom, grows narrower all the way to the top, which terminates in a point. The river Indus, whofe fource is not far from this place, flows at the bottom, its fides being perpendicular, and high; and on the other fide were vaft moraffes, which it was neceffary to fill up before the rock could be taken. Very happily for the Macedonians, they were near a foreft. This the king had cut down, commanding his foldiers to carry off nothing but the trunks, the branches of which were lopped, in order that they might be carried with the lefs difficulty; and he himfelf

threw the first trunk into the morass. The army seeing this, shouted for joy, and every soldier labouring with incredible diligence, the work was finished in seven days; immediately after which the attack began. The officers were of opinion, that it would not be proper for the king to expose himself on this occasion, the danger being evidently too great. However, the trumpet no sooner sounded, but this prince, who was not master of his courage, commanded his guards to follow, himself first climbing the rock. At this sight it appeared no longer inaccessible, and every one flew after him. Never were soldiers exposed to greater danger; many fell from the rock into the river, whose whirlpools swallowed them up. The Barbarians rolled great stones on the foremost, who being scarce able to keep upon their feet (the rock was so slippery) fell down the precipices, and were dashed to pieces. No sight could possibly be more dismal than this; the king greatly afflicted at the loss of so many brave soldiers, caused a retreat to be sounded. Nevertheless, though he had lost all hopes of taking the place, and was determined to raise the siege, he acted as if he intended to continue it, and accordingly gave orders for bringing forward the towers and other engines. The besieged, by way of insult, made great rejoicings; and continued their festivity for two days and two nights, making the rock, and the whole neighbourhood, echo with the sound of their drums and cymbals. But the third night they were not heard, and the Macedonians were suprised to see every part of the rock illuminated with torches. The king was informed, that the Indians had lighted them to assist their flight, and to guide them the more easily in
those

those precipices, during the obscurity of the night. Immediately the whole army, by Alexander's order, shouted aloud, which terrified the fugitives so much, that several of them fancying they saw the enemy, flung themselves from the top of the rock, and perished miserably. The king having so happily and unexpectedly possessed himself of the rock, in an almost miraculous manner, thanked the gods, and offered sacrifice in their honour.

From hence he marched and took Ecbolimus; and after sixteen days march arrived at the river Indus, where he found that Hephæstion had got all things ready for his passage, pursuant to the orders given him. The king of the country, called Omphis, whose father died some time before, had sent to Alexander to know whether he would give him leave to wear the crown. Notwithstanding the Macedonian told him he might, he nevertheless delayed putting it on till his arrival. He then went to meet him, with his whole army: and when Alexander was advanced pretty near, he pushed forward his horse, came up singly to him, and the king did the same. The Indian then told him by an interpreter, " That he was come to meet him at the head of his " army, in order to deliver up all his forces into " his hands. That he surrendered his person and " his kingdom to a monarch, who, he was sensible, " fought only with the view of acquiring glory, and " dreaded nothing so much as treachery." The king greatly satisfied with the frankness of the Barbarian, gave him his hand, and restored him his kingdoms. He then made Alexander a present of fifty six elephants, and a great number of other animals of prodigious size. Alexander asking him which

were

were most necessary to him, husbandmen or soldiers? he replied, that as he was at war with two kings, the latter were of greatest service to him. These two monarchs were Abisares and Porus, the latter of whom was most powerful, and the dominions of both were situated on the other side of the Hydaspes. Omphis assumed the diadem, and took the name of Taxilus, by which the kings of that country were called. He made magnificent presents to Alexander, who did not suffer himself to be exceeded in generosity.

The next day, ambassadors from Abisares waiting upon the king, surrendered up to him pursuant to the power given them, all the dominions of their sovereign; and after each party had promised fidelity on both sides, they returned back.

Alexander expecting that Porus, astonished with the report of his glory, would not fail to submit to him, sent a message to that prince, as if he had been his vassal, requiring him to pay tribute, and meet him upon the frontiers of his dominions. Porus answered with great coldness, that he would do so, but it should be sword in hand. At the same time, a reinforcement of thirty elephants, which were of great service, were sent to Alexander. He gave the superintendance of his elephants to Taxilus, and advanced as far as the borders of the Hydaspes. Porus was encamped on the other side of it, in order to dispute the passage with him; and had posted at the head of his army eighty-five elephants of a prodigious size, and behind them three hundred chariots, guarded by thirty thousand foot; not having, at most, above seven thousand horse. This prince was mounted on an elephant of a much larger size than any of the rest, and he himself exceeded the usual stature of men; so that, clothed in his armour glittering with gold and silver, he appeared at the same time terrible and majestick. The greatness of his courage equalled that of his stature, and he was as wise and prudent as is possible for the monarch of so barbarous a people to be.

The Macedonians dreaded not only the enemy, but the river they were obliged to pass. It was four furlongs wide (about four hundred fathoms) and so deep in every part, that it looked like a sea, and was no where fordable. It was vastly impetuous, notwithstanding its great breadth; for it rolled with as much violence, as if it had been confined to a narrow channel; and its raging, foaming waves, which broke in many places, discovered that it was full of stones and rocks. However, nothing was so dreadful as the appearance of the shore, which was quite covered with men, horses, and elephants. Those hideous animals stood like so many towers, and the Indians exasperated them, in order that the horrid cry they made might fill the enemy with greater terror. However this could not intimidate an army of men, whose courage was proof against all attacks, and who were animated by an uninterrupted series of prosperities; but then they did not think it would be possible for them, as their barks were so crazy, to surmount the rapidity of the stream, or land with safety.

This river was full of little islands, to which the Indians and Macedonians used to swim, with their arms over their heads; and slight skirmishes were every day fought in the sight of the two kings, who were well pleased to make those small excursions of

their

their refpective forces, and to form a judgment from such fkirmifhes, of the fuccefs of a general battle. There were two young officers in Alexander's army, Egefimachus and Nicanor, men of equal intrepidity, and who, having been ever fuccefsful, defpifed dangers of every kind. They took with them the braveft youths in the whole army : and, with no other weapons than their javelins, fwam to an ifland in which feveral of the enemy were landed; where, with fcarce any other affiftance but their intrepidity, they made a great flaughter. After this bold ftroke, they might have retired with glory, were it poffible for rafhnefs, when fuccefsful, to keep within bounds. But as they waited with contempt, and an infulting air, for thofe who came to fuccour their companions, they were furrounded by a band of foldiers, who had fwam unperceived to the ifland, and overwhelmed with the darts which were fhot from far. Thofe who endeavoured to fave themfelves by fwimming, were either carried away by the waves, or fwallowed up by the whirlpools. The courage of Porus, who faw all this from the fhore, was furprifingly increafed by this fuccefs.

Alexander was in great perplexity; and finding he could not pafs the Hydafpes by force of arms, he therefore refolved to have reconrfe to artifice. Accordingly he caufed his cavalry to attempt feveral times to pafs it in the night, and to fhout as if they really intended to ford the river, all things being prepared for that purpofe. Immediately Porus hurried thither with his elephants, but Alexander continued in battle-array on the bank. This ftratagem having been attempted feveral times, and Porus finding the whole was but mere noife and empty menaces,

naces, he took no farther notice of these motions, and only sent scouts to every part of the shore. Alexander, being now no longer apprehensive of having the whole army of the enemy fall upon him, in his attempting to cross the river in the night, began to resolve seriously to pass it.

There was in this river, at a considerable distance from Alexander's camp, an island of greater extent than any of the rest. This being covered with trees, was very proper for him to cover and conceal his design, and therefore he resolved to attempt the passage that way. However, the better to conceal the knowledge of it from the enemy, and deceive them on this occasion, he left Craterus in his camp with a great part of the army, with orders for them to make a great noise, at a certain time which should be appointed, in order to alarm the Indians, and make them believe that he was preparing to cross the river; but that he would not attempt this, till such time as Porus should have raised his camp, and marched away his elephants, either to withdraw or advance towards those Macedonians who should attempt the passage. Between the camp and the island, he had posted Meleager and Gorgias, with the foreign horse and foot, with orders for them to pass over in bodies, the instant they should see him engaged in battle.

After giving these orders, he took the rest of his army, as well cavalry as infantry; and, wheeling off from the shore, in order to avoid being perceived, he advanced in the night time towards the island into which he was resolved to go; and the better to deceive the enemy, Alexander caused his tent to be pitched in the camp where he had left Craterus,
which

which was opposite to that of Porus. His lifeguards were drawn up round, in all the pomp and splendour with which the majesty of a great king is usually surrounded. He also caused a royal robe to be put upon Atalus, who was of the same age with himself, and so much resembled the king, both in stature and features, especially at so great a distance as the breadth of the river, that the enemy might suppose Alexander himself was on the bank, and was attempting the passage of that place. He however was by this time got to the island above-mentioned, and immediately landed upon it from the boats, with the rest of his troops, whilst the enemy was employed in opposing Craterus. But now a furious storm arose, which seemed as if it would retard the execution of his project, yet proved of advantage to it; for so fortunate was this prince, that obstacles changed into advantages, and succours in his favour: the storm was succeeded by a very violent shower, with impetuous winds, flashes of lightning and thunder, insomuch that there was no hearing or seeing any thing. Any man but Alexander would have abandoned his design; but he, on the contrary, was animated by danger, not to mention that the noise, the confusion, and the darkness, assisted his passage. He thereupon made the signal for the embarkation of his troops, and went off himself in the first boat. It is reported, that it was on this occasion he cried out, "O Athenians, could you think I would expose myself to such dangers, to merit your applause!" And, indeed, nothing could contribute more to eternize his name, than the having his actions recorded by such great historians as Thucydides and Xenophon; and so anxious was he about the character which would be given him after his death, that he wifhed it were poffible for him to return again into the world only fo long as was neceffary to know what kind of impreffion the perufal of his hiftory made on the minds of men.

Scarce any perfon appeared to oppofe their defcent, becaufe Porus was wholly taken up with Craterus, and imagined he had nothing to do but to oppofe his paffage. Immediately this general, purfuant to his orders, made a prodigious clamour, and feemed to attempt the paffage of the river. Upon this, all the boats came to fhore, one excepted, which the waves dafhed to pieces againft a rock. The moment Alexander was landed, he drew up in order of battle his little army, confifting of fix thoufand foot and five thoufand horfe. He himfelf headed the latter; and, having commanded the foot to make all imaginable difpatch after him, he marched before. It was his firm opinion, that in cafe the Indians fhould oppofe him with their whole force, his cavalry would give him infinite advantage over them; and that, be this as it would, he might eafily continue fighting till his foot fhould come up; or, that in cafe the enemy, alarmed at the news of his paffing, fhould fly, it would then be in his power to purfue, and make a great flaughter of them.

Porus, upon hearing that Alexander had paffed the river, had fent againft him a detachment, commanded by one of his fons, of two thoufand horfe, and one hundred and twenty chariots. Alexander imagined them at firft to be the enemy's van-guard, and that the whole army was behind them; but, being informed it was but a detachment, he charged them with fuch vigour, that Porus's fon was killed

upon

upon the spot, with four hundred horses, and all the chariots were taken. Each of these chariots carried six men; two were armed with bucklers, two bowmen sat on each side, and two guided the chariot, who nevertheless always fought when the battle grew warm, having a great number of darts, which they discharged at the enemy. But all these did little execution that day, because the rain, which fell in great abundance, had moistened the earth to such a degree, that the horses could scarce stand upon their legs; and the chariots being very heavy, most of them sunk very deep into the mud.

Porus, upon receiving advice of the death of his son, the defeat of the detachment, and of Alexander's approach, was in doubt whether it would be proper for him to continue in his post, because Craterus, with the rest of the Macedonian army, made a feint as if they intended to pass the river. However, he at last resolved to go and meet Alexander, whom he justly supposed to be at the head of the choicest troops of his army. Accordingly, leaving only a few elephants in his camp, to amuse those who were posted on the opposite shore, he set out with thirty thousand foot, four thousand horse, three thousand chariots, and two hundred elephants. Being come into a firm, sandy soil, in which his horses and chariots might wheel about with ease, he drew up his army in battle-array, with an intent to wait the coming up of the enemy. He posted in front, and on the first line, all the elephants at an hundred feet distance one from the other, in order that they might serve as a bulwark to his foot, who were behind. It was his opinion, that the enemy's cavalry would not dare to engage in those intervals, because of the fear those

horses

horses would have of the elephants; and much less the infantry, when they should see that of the enemy posted behind the elephants, and in danger of being trod to pieces by those animals. He had posted some of his foot on the same line with the elephants, in order to cover their right and left; and this infantry was covered by his two wings of horse, before which the chariots were posted. Such was the order and disposition of Porus's army.

Alexander being come in sight of the enemy, waited the coming up of his foot, which marched with the utmost diligence, and arrived a little after: and, in order that they might have time to take breath, and not be led, as they were very much fatigued, against the enemy, he caused his horse to make a great many evolutions, in order to gain time. But now every thing being ready, and the infantry having sufficiently recovered their vigour, Alexander gave the signal of battle. He did not think proper to begin by attacking the enemy's main body, where the infantry and the elephants were posted, for the very reason which had made Porus draw them up in that manner: but his cavalry being stronger, he drew out the greatest part of them; and marching against the left wing, sent Camus with his own regiment of horse, and that of Demetrius, to charge them at the same time; ordering him to attack the cavalry on the left, behind, during which he himself would charge them both in front and flank. Seleucus, Antigonus, and Tauron, who commanded the foot, were ordered not to stir from their posts, till Alexander's cavalry had put that of the enemy, as well as their foot, into disorder.

Being

Being come within arrow-shot, he detached a thousand bowmen on horseback, with orders for them to make their discharge on the horse of Porus's left wing, in order to throw it into disorder, whilst he himself should charge this body in flank, before it had time to rally. The Indians, having joined again their squadrons, and drawn them up into a narrower compass, advanced against Alexander. At that instant Cœnus charged them in the rear, according to the orders given him; insomuch that the Indians were obliged to face about on all sides, to defend themselves from the thousand bowmen, and against Alexander and Cœnus. Alexander, to make the best of the confusion into which this sudden attack had thrown them, charged with great vigour those that made head against him, who being no longer able to stand so violent an attack, were soon broke, and retired behind the elephants, as to an impregnable rampart. The leaders of the elephants made them advance against the enemy's horse; but, that very instant, the Macedonian phalanx moving on a sudden, surrounded those animals, and charged with their pikes the elephants themselves and their leaders. This battle was very different from all those which Alexander had hitherto fought; for the elephants rushing upon the battalions, broke, with inexpressible fury, the thickest of them; when the Indian horse, seeing the Macedonian foot stopped by the elephants, returned to the charge; however, that of Alexander being stronger, and having greater experience in war, broke this body a second time, and obliged it to retire towards the elephants; upon which the Macedonian horse being all united in one body, spread terror and confusion wherever they attacked.

The elephants being all covered with wounds, and the greatest part having lost their leaders, they did not observe their usual order; but, distracted as it were with pain, no longer distinguished friends from foes, but running about from place to place, they overthrew every thing that came in their way. The Macedonians, who had purposely left a greater interval between their battalions, either made way for them wherever they came forward, or charged with darts those that fear and the tumult obliged to retire. Alexander, after having surrounded the enemy with his horse, made a signal to his foot to march up with all imaginable speed, in order to make a last effort, and to fall upon them with his whole force, all which they executed very successfully. In this manner the greatest part of the Indian cavalry were cut to pieces; and a body of their foot, which sustained no loss, seeing themselves charged on all sides, at last fled. Craterus, who had continued in the camp with the rest of his army, seeing Alexander engaged with Porus, crossed the river, and charging the routed soldiers with his troops, who were cool and vigorous, by that means killed as many enemies in the retreat, as had fallen in the battle.

The Indians lost on this occasion twenty thousand foot and three thousand horse; not to mention the chariots which were all broke to pieces, and the elephants that were either killed or taken. Porus's two sons fell in this battle, with Spitacus, governor of the province; all the colonels of horse and foot, and those who guided the elephants and chariots. As for Alexander, he lost but fourscore of the six thousand soldiers who were at the first charge, ten bowmen of the horse, twenty of his horse-guards, and two hundred common soldiers.   Porus,

Porus, after having performed all the duty both of a foldier and a general in the battle, and fought with incredible bravery, feeing all his horfe defeated, and the greateft part of his foot, did not behave like the great Darius, who, on a like difafter, was the firſt that fled; on the contrary, he continued in the field, as long as one battalion or fquadron ftood their ground; but at laft, having received a wound in the fhoulder, he retired upon his elephant : and was eafily diftinguifhed from the reft, by the greatnefs of his ftature, and his unparalleled bravery. Alexander finding who he was by thofe glorious marks, and being defirous of faving this king, fent Taxilus after him, becaufe he was of the fame nation. The latter advancing as near to him as he might, without running any danger of being wounded, called out to him to ftop, in order to hear the meffage he had brought him from Alexander. Porus turning back, and feeing it was Taxilus, his old enemy; How! fays he, is it not Taxilus that calls, that traitor to his country and kingdom. Immediately after which, he would have transfixed him with his dart, had he not inftantly retired. Notwithftandiug this, Alexander was ftill defirous to fave fo brave a prince, and thereupon difpatched their officers, among whom was Meroe, one of his intimate friends, who befought him, in the ftrongeft terms, to wait upon a conqueror, altogether worthy of him. After much intreaty, Porus confented, and accordingly fet forward. Alexander, who had been told of his coming, advanced forward in order to receive him with fome of his train. Being come pretty near, Alexander ftopped, purpofely to take a view of his ftature and noble mein, he being about five cubits in height. Porus did

did not seem dejected at his misfortune, but came up with a resolute countenance, like a valiant warrior, whose courage in defending his dominions ought to acquire him the esteem of the brave prince who had taken him prisoner. Alexander spoke first, and with an august and gracious air, asked him how he desired to be treated? like a king, replied Porus. But, continued Alexander, do you ask nothing more? No, replied Porus; all things are included in that single word. Alexander, struck with this greatness of soul, the magnanimity of which seemed heightened by distress, did not only restore him his kingdom, but annexed other provinces to it, and treated him with the highest testimonies of honour, esteem, and friendship. Porus also continued faithful till his death.

SECT. XV. *Alexander advances into India. Resolves to march as far as the Ganges, which raises a general discontent in his army. Remonstrances being made to him on that account, he lays aside his design, and is contented with going no farther than the ocean. He subdues all things in his way thither, and is exposed to great danger at the siege of the city of the Oxydracae; and arriving at last at the ocean, he afterwards prepares for his return into Europe.*

ALEXANDER, after his famous victory over Porus, advanced into India, where he subdued a great many nations and cities. He looked upon himself as a conqueror by profession as well as by his dignity, and engaged every day in new exploits with so much
ardour

ardour and vivacity, that he seemed to fancy himself invested with a personal commission, and that there was an immediate obligation upon him to storm all cities, to lay waste all provinces, to extirpate all nations, which should refuse his yoke; and that he should have considered himself as guilty of a crime, had he forebore visiting every corner of the earth, and carrying terror and desolation wherever he went. He passed the Acesines, and afterwards the Hydraotes, two considerable rivers. Advice was then brought him that a great number of free Indians had made a confederacy to defend their liberties; and among the rest, the Caytheans, who were the most valiant and the most skilful of those nations in the art of war; and that they were encamped near a strong city, called Sangala. Alexander set out against those Indians, defeated them in a pitched battle, took the city, and razed it to the very foundations.

This prince being determined to continue the war as long as he should meet with new nations, and to look upon them as enemies whilst they should live independent on him, was meditating about passing the Hyphasus. He was told, that after passing that river he must travel eleven days through desarts, and that then he would arrive at the Ganges, the greatest river in all India. That farther in the country lived the Gangarida, and the Prasii, whose king was preparing to oppose his entering his dominions, at the head of twenty thousand horse, and two hundred thousand foot, reinforced by two thousand chariots; and, which struck the greatest terror, with three thousand elephants. A report of this being spread through the army, surprised all the soldiers, and raised a general murmer. The Macedonians, who, after having travelled through so many countries, and being grown grey in the field, were incessantly directing their eyes and wishes toward their dear, native country, made loud complaints, that Alexander should every day heap war upon war, and danger on danger. They had undergone, but just before, inexpressible fatigues, for above two months. Some bewailed their calamities in such terms as raised compassion; others insolently cried aloud, that they would go no farther.

Alexander, being informed of this tumult, immediately sent for the officers into his tent, and commanded them to assemble his whole army together, he then addressed them in the most lively and pathetick language, begging they would not abandon him in the midst of his career to glory. But finding it would be impossible to change the resolution of the soldiers, he commanded them to prepare for their return. This news filled the whole army with inexpressible joy: and Alexander never appeared greater, or more glorious, than on this day, in which he designed, for the sake of his subjects, to sacrifice some part of his glory and grandeur. The whole camp echoed with praise and blessings of Alexander, for having suffered himself to be overcome by his own army, who was invincible to the rest of the world.

Alexander had not spent above three or four months in conquering all the country between the Indus and Hyphasess, called to this day Pengab, that is, the five waters, from the five rivers which compose it. Before his setting out, he raised twelve altars, to serve as so many trophies and thanksgivings for the victories he had obtained.

He

He afterwards passed the Hydraotes, and left Porus all the lands he had conquered, as far as the Hyphæsus. He also reconciled this monarch with Taxilus, and settled a peace between them by means of an alliance, equally advantageous to both. From thence he went and encamped on the banks of the Acesines; but great rains having made this river overflow its banks, and the adjacent countries being under water, he was obliged to remove his camp higher up. Here a fit of sickness carried off Cœnus, whose loss was bewailed by the king and the whole army. There was not a greater officer among the Macedonians, and he had distinguished himself in a very peculiar manner in every battle in which he engaged. But now Alexander was preparing for his departure.

His fleet consisted of eight hundred vessels, as well gallies as boats, to carry the troops and provisions. Every thing being ready, the whole army embarked, about the setting of the Pleiades or seven stars, according to Aristobulus, that is, about the end of October. The fifth day the fleet arrived where the Hydaspes and Acesines mix their streams. Here the ships were very much shattered, because these rivers unite with such prodigious rapidity, that as great storms arise in this part, as in the open sea. At last he came into the country of the Oxydracæ and the Malli, the most valiant people in those parts. These were perpetually at war one with another; but having united for their mutual safety, they had drawn together ten thousand horse, and fourscore thousand foot, all vigorous young men, with nine hundred chariots. However, Alexander defeated them in several engagements, dispossessed them of
some

some strong holds, and at last marched against the city of the Oxydracœ, whither the greatest part were retired. Immediately he causes the scaling-ladders to be set up; and, as they were not nimble enough for Alexander, he forces one of the scaling-ladders from a soldier; runs up the first (covered with his shield) and gets to the top of the wall, followed only by Peucestes and Limneus. The soldiers, believing him to be in danger, mounted swiftly to succour him; but the ladders breaking, the king was left alone. Alexander, seeing himself the butt, against which all the darts were levelled, both from the towers and from the ramparts, was so rash, rather than valiant, as to leap into the city, which was crowded with the enemy, having nothing to expect, but to be either taken or killed before it would be possible for him to rise, and without once having an opportunity to defend himself, or revenge his death. But, happily for him, he poised his body in such a manner, that he fell upon his feet; and finding himself standing, sword in hand, he repulsed such as were nearest him, and even killed the general of the enemy who advanced to run him through. Happily for him a second time, not far from thence there stood a great tree, against the trunk of which he leaned, his shield receiving all the darts that were shot at him from a distance; for no one dared to approach him, so great was the dread which the boldness of the enterprise, and the fire that shot from his eyes, had struck into the enemy. At last an Indian let fly an arrow three feet long (that being the length of their arrows) which piercing his coat of mail, entered a considerable way into his body, a little above the right side. So great a quantity of blood issued from the wound, that he dropped his arms, and lay as dead.

dead. Behold then this mighty conqueror, this vanquisher of nations, upon the point of losing his life, not at the head of his armies, but in a corner of an obscure city, into which his rashness had thrown him. The Indian who had wounded Alexander, ran, in the greatest transports of joy, to strip him; however, Alexander no sooner felt the hand of his enemy upon him, but, fired with the thirst of revenge, he recalled his spirits; and, laying hold of the Indian, as he had no arms, he plunged his dagger into his side. Some of his chief officers, as Peucestes, Leonatus, and Timæus, who had got to the top of the wall with some soldiers, came up that instant, and attempting impossibilities, for the sake of saving their sovereign's life, they form themselves as a bulwark round his body, and sustain the whole effort of the enemy. It was then that a mighty battle was fought round him. In the mean time the soldiers, who climbed up with the officers above mentioned, having broke the bolts of a little gate standing between two towers, they, by that means, let in the Macedonians. Soon after the town was taken, and all the inhabitants were put to the sword, without distinction of age or sex. The first care they took was to carry Alexander into his tent; being got into it, the surgeons cut off, so very dexterously, the wood of the shaft, which had been shot into his body, that they did not move the steel point; and after undressing him, they found it was a bearded arrow; and that it could not be pulled out, without danger unless the wound was widened. The king bore the operation with incredible resolution, so that there was no occasion for people to hold him. The incision being made, and the arrow drawn out, so great.

great an effusion of blood ensued, that the king fainted away. Every one thought him dead; but the blood being stopped, he recovered by degrees, and knew the persons about him, all that day, and the whole night after, the army continued under arms round his tent; and would not stir from their posts, till certain news was brought of his being better, and that he began to take a little rest.

At the end of the seven days he had employed for his recovery, before his wound was closed, as he knew that the report of his death increased among the Barbarians, he caused two vessels to be joined together, and had his tent pitched in the middle, in sight of every one; purposely to shew himself to those who may imagine him dead, and to ruin, by this means, all their projects, and the hopes with which they flattered themselves. He afterwards went down the river, going before at some distance from the rest of the fleet, for fear least the noise of the oars should keep him from sleep, which he wanted very much. When he was a little better and able to go out, the soldiers who were upon guard, brought him his litter, but he refused it, and calling for his horse, mounted him. At this sight, all the shore, and the neighboring forests echoed with the acclamations of the army, who imagined they saw him rise, in a manner from the grave. Being come near his tent, he alighted, and walked a little way, surrounded with a great number of soldiers, some of whom kissed his hands, whilst others clasped his knees; others again were contented with only touching his clothes, and with seeing him; but all in general burst into tears, and calling for a thousand blessings

blessings from heaven, wished him long life, and an uninterrupted series of prosperity.

At this instant deputies came from the Malli, with the chiefs of the Oxydracœ, being one hundred and sixty, besides the governors of the cities and of the province, who brought him presents, and paid him homage, pleading in excuse for not having done it before, their strong love of liberty. They declared, that they were ready to receive for their governor, whomsoever he pleased to nominate; that they would pay him tribute, and give him hostages. He demanded a thousand of the chief persons of their nations, whom he also might make use of in war, till he had subjected all the country. They put into his hands such of their countrymen as were handsomest and best shaped, with five hundred chariots, though not demanded by him; at which the king was so much pleased, that he gave them back their hostages, and appointed Philip their governor.

Alexander, who was overjoyed at this embassy, and found his strength increase daily, tasted with so much the greater pleasure the fruits both of his victory and health, as he had like to have lost them forever. His chief courtiers, and most intimate friends, thought it a proper juncture, during this calm and serenity of his mind, for them to unbosom themselves, and expose their fears to him, which they expressed in the most pathetic language, and begged of the king to be more careful of so precious a life, if not for his own sake, at least for theirs, and for the felicity of the universe.

Alexander was strongly touched with these testimonies of their affection, and having embraced them severally with inexpressible tenderness, he answered

as

as follows: "I cannot enough thank all present,
"who are the flower of my citizens and friends, not
"only for your having this day, preferred my safety
"to your own, but also for the strong proofs you
"have given me of your zeal and affection, from
"the beginning of this war, and if any thing is capa-
"ble of making me wish for a longer life, it is the
"pleasure of enjoying, for years to come, such val-
"uable friends as you. But give me leave to ob-
"serve, that in some cases we differ very much in
"opinion. You wish to enjoy me long; and even,
"if it were possible, for ever; but as to myself, I
"compute the length of my existence, not by years,
"but by glory. I might have confined my ambi-
"tion within the narrow limits of Macedonia; and,
"contented with the kingdom my ancestors left me
"have waited, in the midst of pleasures and indo-
"lence, an inglorious old age. I own, that if my
"victories, not my years are computed, I shall
"seem to have lived long; but can you imagine,
"that after having made Europe and Asia but one
"empire, after having conquered the two noblest
"parts of the world, in the tenth year of my reign,
"and the thirtieth of my age, that it will become
"me to stop in the midst of so exalted a career,
"and discontinue the pursuit of glory, to which I
"have entirely devoted myself; know, that this
"glory enobles all things, and gives a true and solid
"grandeur to whatever appears insignificant; in
"what place soever I may fight, I shall fancy myself
"upon the stage of the world, and in presence of all
"mankind. I confess that I have atchieved migh-
"ty things hitherto; but the country we are now
"in, reproaches me that a woman has done still
                                    "greater.

" greater. It is Semeramis I mean. How many
" nations did she conquer! How many cities were
" built by her! what magnificent and stupenduous
" works did she furnish! How shameful is it, that
" I should not yet have attained to so exalted a pitch
" of glory; do but second my ardour and I shall
" soon surpass her; defend me only from secret
" cabals, and domestic traitors, by which most
" princes lose their lives. I take the rest upon my-
" self, and will be answerable to you for all the
" events of the war."

Alexander, after having ended his speech, dismissed the assembly, and continued encamped for several days in this place. He afterwards went upon the river, and his army marched after him upon the banks. He then came among the Sabracae a powerful nation of Indians. These had levied sixty thousand foot, and six thousand horse, and reinforced them with five hundred chariots; however, the arrival of Alexander spread a terror through the whole country, and accordingly they sent ambassadors to make their submission. After having built another city, which he also called Alexandria, he arrived in the territories of Musicanus, a very rich prince, and afterwards in those of the king of Samus. At the siege of one of this kings towns, Ptolemy was dangerously wounded; for the Indians had poisoned all their arrows and swords so that the wounds they made were mortal. Alexander, who had the highest love and esteem for Ptolemy, was very much afflicted, and caused him to be brought in his bed near him, that he himself might have an eye to his cure. He was his near relation, and according to some writers, a natural son of Philip. Ptolemy was one of the bravest

bravest in the army, was highly esteemed in war, and had greater talents for peace. He was averse to luxury, vastly generous, easy of access, and did not imitate the pomp, which wealth and prosperity had made the rest of the Macedonian noblemen assume ; in a word it is hard to say, whether he were more esteemed by his sovereign, or his country. We are told, there appeared to him in a dream a dragon, which presented him an herb, as an effectual remedy ; and that upon his waking, he ordered it to be sent for ; when laying it upon the wound, it was healed in a few days, to the universal joy of the army.

The king continuing his voyage, arrived at Patala, about the beginning of the dog-days, that is, about the end of July ; so that the fleet was nine months at least from its setting out, till its arrival at that place. There the river Indus divides into two large arms, and forms an Island, Alexander caused a citadel to be built in Patala, as also an harbor and an arsenal for the shipping. This being done, he embarked on the right arm of the river, in order to sail as far as the ocean, exposing in this manner so many brave men to the mercy of a river with which they are wholly unacquainted. The only consolation they had in this rash enterprize, was Alexander's uninterrupted success. When he had sailed twenty leagues, the pilots told him that they began to perceive the sea-air, and therefore believed that the ocean could not be far off. Upon this news, leaping for joy, he besought the sailors to row with all their strength, and told the soldiers, " That they at last were come
" to the end of their toils, which they had so earnest-
" ly desired ; that now nothing could oppose their
" valour, nor add to their glory ; that without fight-
" ing

" ing any more, or spilling of blood, they were
" masters of the universe, that their exploits had
" the same boundaries with nature; and that they
" would be spectators of things, known only to the
" immortal gods."

Being come nearer the sea, a circumstance new and unheard of by the Macedonians, threw them into the utmost confusion, and exposed the fleet to the greatest danger; and this was the ebbing and flowing of the ocean. Forming a judgment of this vast sea, from that of the Mediteranean, the only one they knew, and whose ebbings are imperceptable, they were very much astonished when they saw it rise to a great height, and overflow the country; and considered it as a mark of anger of the gods, to punish their rashness. They were no less surprized and terrified, some hours after, when they saw the ebbing of the sea, which now withdrew as it had before advanced, leaving those lands uncovered, it had so lately overflowed. The fleet was very much shattered, and the ships being now upon dry land, the fields were covered with clothes, with broken oars and planks, as after a great storm.

At last Alexander, after having sailed full nine months in rivers, arrived at the ocean, where gazing with the utmost eagerness upon that vast expanse of waters, he imagined that this sight, worthy so great a conqueror as himself, greatly overpaid all the toils he had undergone, and the many thousand men he had lost to arrive at it. He then offered sacrifices to the gods, and particularly to Neptune; threw into the sea the bulls he had slaughtered, and a great number of golden cups, and besought the gods not to suffer any mortal after him, to exceed the bounds of of his expedition. Finding that he had extended his conquests to the extremities of the earth on that side, he imagined he had completed his mighty design; and, highly delighted with himself, he returned to rejoin the rest of his fleet and army, which waited for him at Patala, and in the neighbourhood of it.

SECT. XVI. *Alexander, in his march through deserts, is grievously distressed by famine. He arrives at Pasagardae, where Cyrus's monument stood. Orsines, a powerful lord, is put to death by the clandestine intrigues of Bagoas the eunuch. Calaus the Indian ascends a funeral pile, where he puts himself to death. Alexander marries Statira, the daughter of Darius. Harpalus arrives at Athens; Demosthenes is banished. The Macedonian soldiers make an insurrection, which Alexander appeases. He recalls Antipater from Macedonia, and sends Craterus in his room. The king's sorrow for the death of Hephaestion.*

ALEXANDER being returned to Patala, prepared all things for the departure of his fleet. He appointed Nearchus admiral of it, who was the only officer that had the courage to accept of this commission, which was a very hazardous one, because they were to sail over a sea entirely unknown to them. The king was very much pleased at his accepting of it; and, after testifying his acknowledgement upon that account in the most obliging terms, he commanded him to take the best ship.

ships in the fleet, and to go and found the sea-coast extending from the Indus to the bottom of the Persian gulph: and, after having given these orders, he set out by land for Babylon.

Nearchus did not leave the Indus at the same time with Alexander. It was not yet the season proper for sailing. It was summer, when the southern sea-winds rise; and the season of the northwinds, which blow in winter, was not yet come. He therefore did not set sail till about the end of September, which was too soon; and accordingly he was incommoded by winds some days after his departure, and obliged to shelter himself for twenty-four days.

We are obliged for these particulars to Arrian, who has given us an exact journal of this voyage, copied from that of Nearchus the admiral.

Alexander, after having left Patala, marched thro' the country of the Oritœ, the capital whereof was called Ora or Rhambacis. Here he was in such want of provision, that he lost a great number of soldiers, and brought back from India scarce the fourth part of his army, which had consisted of an hundred and twenty thousand foot, and fifteen thousand horse. Sickness had swept them away in multitudes; but famine made a still greater havock among the troops in this barren country, which was neither ploughed nor sowed; its inhabitants being savages, who fared very hard, and led a most uncomfortable life. After they had eaten all the palm-tree roots that could be met with, they were obliged to feed upon the beasts of burthen, and next upon their war-horses; and when they had no beasts left to carry their baggage, they were forced to burn those rich spoils, for the sake of which the Macedonians had run to the extremities

tremities of the earth. The plague, a disease which generally accompanies famine, completed the calamity of the soldiers, and destroyed great numbers of them.

After marching threescore days, Alexander arrived on the confines of Gadrosia, where he found plenty of all things; for the soil was not only very fruitful, but the kings and great men, who lay nearest that country, sent him all kinds of provisions. He continued some time here, in order to refresh his army. The governors of India having sent, by his order, a great number of horses, and all kinds of beasts of burthen, from the several kingdoms subject to him, he remounted his troops; equipped those who had lost every thing; and soon after presented all of them with arms, as beautiful as those they had before, which it was very easy for him to do, as they were upon the confines of Persia, at that time in peace, and in a very flourishing condition.

He arrived in Carmania, now called Kerman, and went through it, not with the air and equipage of a warrior and a conqueror, but in a kind of masquerade, and bacchanalian festivity, committing the most riotous and extravagant actions. He was drawn by eight horses, himself being seated on a magnificent chariot, above which a scaffold was raised, in the form of a square stage, where he passed the days and nights in feasts and carousing. This chariot was preceded and followed by an infinite number of others, some of which in the shape of tents, were covered with rich carpets, and purple coverlets; and others, shaped like cradles, were overshadowed with branches of trees. On the sides of the roads, and at the doors of houses, a great number of casks ready

ready broached were placed, whence the soldiers drew wine in large flaggons, cups, and goblets, prepared for that purpose.

The whole country echoed with the sound of instruments, and the howling of bacchanals, who, with their hair dishevelled, and like so many frantick creatures, ran up and down, abandoning themselves in every kind of licentiousness. All this he did in imitation of the triumph of Bacchus, who, as we are told, crossed all Asia in this equipage, after he had conquered India. This riotous, dissolute march lasted seven days, during all which time the army was never sober. It was very happy, says Quintius Curtius, for them, that the conquered nations did not think of attacking them in this condition; for a thousand resolute men, well armed, might with great ease have defeated these conquerors of the world, whilst thus plunged in wine and excess.

Nearchus still keeping along the sea-coasts, from the mouth of the Indus, came at last into the Persian gulph, and arrived at the island of Harmusia, now called Ormus. He there was informed, that Alexander was not above five days journey from him. Having left the fleet in a secure place, he went to meet Alexander, accompanied only by four persons. The king was very anxious about his fleet. When news was brought him that Nearchus was arrived almost alone, he imagined that it had been entirely destroyed, and that Nearchus had been so very happy as to escape from the general defeat. His arrival confirmed him still more in his opinion, when he beheld a company of pale, lean creatures, whose countenances were so much changed, that it was scarce possible to know them again. Taking Nearchus aside,

aside, he told him, that he was overjoyed at his return, but at the same time was inconsolable for the loss of his fleet. Your fleet, royal sir, cried he immediately, thanks to the gods, is not lost. Upon which he related the condition in which he left it. Alexander could not refrain from tears, and confessed, that this happy news gave him greater pleasure than the conquest of all Asia. He heard, with uncommon delight, the account Nearchus gave of his voyage, and the discoveries he had made; and bid him return back, and go quite up the Euphrates as far as Babylon, pursuant to the first orders he had given him.

In Carmania, many complaints were made to Alexander, concerning governors and other officers, who had grievously oppressed the people of various provinces during his absence: for, fully persuaded he would never return, they had exercised every species of rapine, tyranny, cruelty and oppression. But Alexander strongly affected with their grievances, put to death as many as were found guilty of maladministration, and with them six hundred soldiers, who had been the instruments of their exactions, and other crimes. He afterwards treated with the same severity, all such of his officers as were convicted of the like guilt, so that his government was beloved by all the conquered nations.

The great pleasure Alexander took, in the account which Nearchus gave him of his successful voyage, made that prince have a great inclination to go upon the ocean. He proposed no less than to sail from the Persian gulph, round Arabia and Africa, and to return into the Mediterranean by the Straits of Gibralter, called at that time Hercules's pillars.

a voyage

a voyage which had been several times attempted, and once performed, by order of a king of Egypt, called Nchao. It was afterwards his design, when he should have humbled the pride of Carthage, against which he was greatly exasperate, to cross into Spain, called by the Greeks Iberia; he next was to go over the Alps, and coast along Italy, where he would have but a short passage into Epirus, and from thence into Macedonia. For this purpose, he sent orders to the viceroys of Mesopotamia, and Syria, to build in several parts of the Euphrates, and particularly at Thaspacus, ships sufficient for that enterprise; and he caused to be felled, on mount Libanus, a great number of trees, which were to be carried into the above mentioned city. But this project, as well as a great many others which he meditated, were all defeated by his early death.

Continuing his march, he went to Passagardæ, a city of Persia. Orsines was governor of the country, and the greatest nobleman in it, being descended from Cyrus. He had done Alexander a signal piece of service. The person, who governed the provinces during Alexanders expedition into India, happened to die; when Orsines observing, that, for want of a governor, all things were running to confusion, took the administration upon himself, composed matters very happily, and preserved them in the utmost tranquility, till Alexander's arrival. He went to meet him, with presents of all kinds, for himself as well as his officers. These consisted of a great number of fine managed horses, chariots, jewels, gold vases of a prodigious weight, purple robes, and four thousand talents of silver. However this generous magnificence proved fatal to him; for he

presented

presented such gifts to the principal grandees of the court, as infinitely exceeded their expectations, but gave nothing to the eunuch Bagoas, the king's favourite; and this not through forgetfulness, but out of contempt. Some persons telling him how much the king loved Bagoas, he answered, "I honor the king's friends, but not an infamous eunuch." These words being told Bagoas, he employed all his credit to ruin a prince descended from the noblest blood in the east, and irreproachable in his conduct. He even bribed some of Orsines attendants, giving them instructions how to impeach him at a proper season; and in the mean time, wherever he was alone with the king, he filled his mind with suspicions and distrust, by perpetually charging him either with exactions or treason.

Bagoas after having taken his measures at distance, at last gave birth to his dark design. Alexander, having caused the monument of Cyrus to be opened, in order to perform funeral honours to the ashes of that great prince, found nothing in it, but an old rotten shield, two Scythian bows, and a scymitar; whereas he hoped to find it full of gold and silver, as the Persians had reported. The king laid a golden crown on his urn, and covered it with his cloak; vastly surprised that so powerful and renowned a prince had not been buried with greater pomp than a private man. Bagoas thinking this a proper time for him to speak, "Are we to wonder, (says he) " to find the tombs of kings so empty since the " houses of governors of provinces are filled with " the gold of which they have deprived them? I, " indeed, had never seen this monument; but I " have heard Darius say, that immense treasures

were

" were buried in it. Hence flowed the unbounded
" liberality and profusion of Orsines, who, by be-
" stowing what he could not keep, without ruining
" himself, thought to make a merit of this in your
" fight." This charge was without the least foundation; and yet the Magi, who guarded the sepulchre, were put to the torture, but all to no purpose; and nothing was discovered relating to the pretended theft. Their silence, on this occasion, ought naturally to have cleared Orsines; but the artful, insinuating discourses of Bagoas, had made a deep impression on Alexander's mind, and by that means given calumny an easy access to it. The accusers, whom Bagoas had suborned, having made choice of a favourable moment, came and impeached Orsines, and charged him with the commission of several odious crimes, and among the rest, with stealing the treasures of the monument. At this charge, the matter appeared no longer doubtful, and the indications were thought sufficient; so that this prince was loaded with chains, before he so much as suspected that any accusation had been brought against him; and was put to death, without being so much as heard, or confronted with his accusers.

From Passagardæ, Alexander came to Persepolis; and, surveying the remains of the conflagration, was exasperated against himself, for his folly in setting it on fire. From hence he advanced towards Susa. Nearchus, in compliance with his orders, had begun to sail up the Euphrates with his fleet; but, upon advice that Alexander was going to Susa, he came down again to the mouth of the Pasi-Tigris, and sailed up this river to a bridge, where Alexander was to pass it. Then the naval and land armies joined.

The

The king offered to his gods sacrifices, by way of thanks for his happy return, and great rejoicings were made in the camp. Nearchus received the honours due to him, for the care he had taken of the fleet; and for having conducted it so far safe, through numberless dangers.

Alexander found in Susa all the captives of quality he had left there. He married Statira, Darius's oldest daughter, and gave the youngest to his dear Hephæstion. And in order that, by making these marriages more common, his own might not be censured, he persuaded the greatest noblemen in his court, and his principal favourites, to imitate him. Accordingly they chose from among the noblest families of Persia, about fourscore young maidens, whom they married. His design was, by these alliances, to cement so strongly the union of the two nations, that they should henceforward form but one, under his empire. The nuptials were solemnized after the Persian manner. He likewise feasted all the rest of the Macedonians who had married before in that country. It is related that there were nine thousand guests at this feast, and that he gave each of them a golden cup for the libations.

Not satisfied with this bounty, he would also pay his soldiers' debts. But finding that several would not declare the sums they owed, for fear of its being an artifice meanly to discover those among them who were too lavish of their money, he appointed in his camp, offices, where all debts were paid without asking the name of either the debtor or creditor. His liberality was very great on this occasion, and gave prodigious satisfaction; we are told that it amounted to near ten thousand talents. But his indulgence,

gence, in permitting every person to conceal his name, was a still more agreeable circumstance. He reproached the soldiers for their seeming to suspect the truth of his promise, and said to them, "That a king ought never to forfeit his word with his subjects; nor his subjects suspect that he could be guilty of so shameful a prevarication."

And now there arrived at Susa, thirty thousand young men, most of the same age, and called Epigones, that is successors; as coming to relieve the old soldiers in their duty and long fatigues. Such only had been made choice of, as were the strongest and best shaped in all Persia; and had been sent to the governors of such cities as were either founded or conquered by Alexander. These had instructed them in military discipline, and in all things relating to the science of war. They were all very neatly dressed, and armed after the Macedonian manner. These came and encamped before the city, where, drawing up in battle-array, they were reviewed; and performed their exercise before the king, who was extremely well pleased, and very bountiful to them afterwards, at which the Macedonians took great umbrage. And indeed Alexander observing these were harrassed and tired out with the length of the war, and often vented murmurs and complaints in the assemblies; he for that reason was desirous of training up these new forces, purposely to check the licentiousness of the veterans. It is dangerous to disgust a whole nation, and to favour foreigners too openly.

In the mean time Harpalus, whom Alexander, during his expedition into India, had appointed governor of Babylon, quitted his service. Flattering himself

himself with hopes that this prince would never return from his wars in that country, he had given a loose to all kinds of licentiousness, and consumed in his infamous revels, part of the wealth with which he had been entrusted. As soon as he was informed that Alexander in his return from India, punished very severely such of his lieutenants as had abused their power, he meditated how he might best secure himself; and for this purpose amassed five thousand talents, that is, about seven hundred and fifty thousand pounds; assembled six thousand soldiers, withdrew into Attica, and landed at Athens.

Immediately all such orators as made a trade of eloquence, ran to him in crowds, all ready to be corrupted by bribes, as they were before by hopes of them. Harpalus did not fail to distribute a small part of his wealth among these orators, to win them over to his interest, but he offered Phocion seven hundred talents, and even put his person under his protection, well knowing the prodigious authority he had over the people.

The fame of his probity, and particularly of his disinterestedness, had gained him this credit. Philip's deputies had offered him great sums of money in that prince's name, and intreating him to accept them, if not for himself, at least for his children, who were so poor, that it would be impossible for them to support the glory of his name: "If they
" resemble me, replied Phocion, the little spot of
" ground, with the prudence of which I h hither-
" to lived, and which has raised   y you
" mention, will be sufficient to m   em; if
" it will not, I do not intend to le   em wealth,
" merely to foment and heighten i   ." Alexander

ander having likewise sent him an hundred talents, Phocion asked those who brought them, upon what design Alexander sent him so great a sum, and did not remit any to the rest of the Athenians? It is replied they, because Alexander looks upon you as the only just and virtuous man. Says Phocion, let him suffer me still to enjoy that character, and be really what I am taken for.

The reader will suppose, that he did not give a more favourable reception to the persons sent by Harpalus. And indeed he spoke to them in very harsh terms, declaring, that he should immediately take such measures as would be disagreeable to the person on whose errand they came, in case he did not leave off bribing the city; the people also, were highly exasperated against Harpalus, and expelled him from the city.

Upon the first report of Harpalus's flying to Athens, Alexander, fully determined to go in person to punish Harpalus and the Athenians, had commanded a fleet to be equipped. But after news was brought that the people in their assembly had ordered him to depart their city, he laid aside all thoughts of returning into Europe.

Alexander, having still a curiosity to see the ocean, came down from Susa, upon the river Eulæus; and after having coasted the Persian gulph to the mouth of the Tygris, he went up that river towards the army, which was encamped on the banks of it, near the city of Opis, under the command of Hephæstion.

Upon his arrival there, he published a declaration in the army, by which all the Macedonians, who, by reason of their age, wounds, or any other infirmity, were unable to support any longer the fatigues of

the

the service, were permitted to return into Greece; declaring, that his design was to discharge them; to be bountiful to them, and send them back to their native country in a safe and honourable manner. His intention was, in making this declaration, to oblige, and at the same time give them the strongest proof how greatly they were in his esteem. However, the very contrary happened: for being already disgusted upon some other accounts, especially by the visible preference which Alexander gave to foreigners, they imagined, that his resolution was to make Asia the seat of his empire, and to disengage himself from the Macedonians; and that the only motive of his doing this, was, that they might make room for the new troops he had levied in the conquered countries. This alone was sufficient to exasperate them to fury. Upon which, without observing the least order or discipline, or regarding the remonstrances of their officers, they went to the king with an air of insolence which they had never assumed till then, and with seditious cries unanimously demanded to be discharged, saying further, that since he despised the soldiers who had gained him all his victories, he and his father Ammon, might carry on the war against whomsoever, and in what manner they pleased; but as for themselves, they were fully determined not to serve him any longer.

 The king, no way surprised, and without once hesitating, jumps from his tribunal; causes the principal mutineers, whom he himself pointed out to his guards, to be immediately seized, and others thirteen to be punished. This bold and vigorous action, which thunderstruck the Macedonians, suppressed their courage in an instant: quite amazed and confounded,

founded, and scarce daring to look at one another, they stood with downcast eyes, and were so dispirited, and trembled so prodigiously, that they were unable either to speak or even to think. Seeing them in this condition, he re-ascended his tribunal, where, after repeating to them, with a severe countenance, and a menacing tone of voice, the numerous favours which Philip his father had bestowed upon them, and all the marks of kindness and friendship by which he himself had distinguished them, he concluded with these words: " You all desire a discharge; " I grant it you. Go now, and publish to the " whole world, that you have left your prince to " the mercy of the nations he had conquered, who " were more affectionate to him than you." After speaking this, he returned suddenly into his tent; cashiers his old guard; appoints another in its place, all composed of Persian soldiers; shuts himself up for some days, and would not see any person all the time.

Had the Macedonians been sentenced to die, it could not have surprised them more than when news was brought them, that the king had confided the guard of his person to the Persians. They could suppress their grief no longer, so that nothing was heard but cries, groans, and lamentations. Soon after, they all run together to the king's tent, threw down their arms, confessed their guilt; acknowledging their fault with tears and sighs; declare that the loss of life will not be so grievous as the loss of honour; and protest that they will not leave the place till the king has pardoned them. At last Alexander could no longer resist the tender proofs they gave of their sorrow and repentance; so that when he himself, at his coming out of his tent, saw them in this dejected condition, he could not refrain from tears; and after some gentle reproaches, which were softened by an air of humanity and kindness, he declared so loud as to be heard by them all, that he restored them to his friendship. This was restoring them to life, as was manifest from their shouts.

He afterwards discharged such Macedonians as were no longer able to carry arms, and sent them back to their native country with rich presents. He commanded, that at the exhibiting of the public games, they should be allowed the chief places in the theatre, and there sit with crowns on their heads; and gave orders, that the children of those who had lost their lives in his service, should receive, during their minority, the same pay which had been given their fathers.

Alexander appointed Craterus commander of these soldiers, to whom he gave the government of Macedonia, Thessala, and Thrace, which Antipater had enjoyed; and the latter was commanded to bring the recruits instead of Craterus. The king had long since been quite tired with the complaints of his mother and Antipater, who could not agree. She charged Antipater of aspiring to sovereign power, and the latter complained of her violent and untractable disposition; and had often declared in his letters, that she did not behave in a manner suitable to her dignity. It was with some reluctance Antipater resigned his government.

(*b*) From Opis, Alexander arrived at Ecbatana, in Media, where, after having dispatched the most
urgent·

(*b*) *A. M.* 3680. *Ant. J. C.* 325.

urgent affairs of the kingdom, he again solemnized games and festivals: there had come to him from Greece, three thousand dancers, makers of machinery, and other persons skilled in diversions of this kind. It happened during the celebration of these festivals, that Hepæstion died of a disease which he brought upon himself. Alexander abandoning himself to immoderate drinking, his whole court followed his example, and sometimes spent whole days and nights in these excesses. In one of them Hephæstion lost his life.

In order to remove, by business and employment, the melancholy ideas which the death of his favourite perpetually awakened in his mind, Alexander marched his army against the Coffæi, a warlike nation inhabiting the Mountains of Media, whom not one of the Persian monarchs had ever been able to conquer. However, the king reduced them in forty days, afterwards passed the Tigris, and marched towards Babylon.

SECT. XVII. *Alexander enters Babylon, contrary to the sinister predictions of the Magi and Soothsayers. He there forms the plan of several voyages and conquests. He sets about repairing the breaches made in the piers of the Tygris and Euphrates, and rebuilding the temple of Balus. He abandons himself to immoderate drinking, which brings him to his end. The universal grief spread over the whole empire upon that account. Sysigambis is not able to survive him. Preparations are made to convey Alexander's corps to the temple of Jupiter-Ammon, in Libya.* ALEXANDER

ALEXANDER being arrived within a league and a half of Babylon, the Chaldeans who pretend to know futurity by the stars, deputed to him some of their old men, to acquaint him, that he would be in danger of his life, in case he entered that city; and were very urgent with him to go on farther. The Babylonish astrologers were held in such great reputation, that this advice made a prodigious impression on his mind, and filled him with confusion and dread. Upon this, after sending several of the grandees of his court to Babylon, he himself went another way; and having marched about ten leagues, he stopped for some time in the place where he had encamped his army. The Greek philosophers, being told the foundation of his fear and scruples, waited upon him; when setting, in the strongest light, the principles of Anaxagoras, whose tenets they followed, they demonstrated to him, in the strongest manner, the vanity of astrology; and made him have so great a contempt for divination in general, and for that of the Chaldeans in particular, that he immediately marched towards Babylon with his whole army. He knew that there were arrived in that city, ambassadors from all parts of the world; who waited for his coming; the whole earth echoing so much with the terror of his name, that the several nations came, with inexpressible ardour to pay homage to Alexander as to him who was to be their sovereign. This view, which agreeably soothed the strongest of all his passions, contributed very much to stifle every other reflection, and to make him careless of all advice that might be given him; so that he set forward with all possible diligence towards that great city, there to hold the states-general, in a manner,

ner, of the world. After making a moft magnificent entry, he gave audience to all the ambaffadors, with the grandeur and dignity fuitable to a great monarch, and, at the fame time, with the affability and politenefs of a prince, who is defirous of winning the affection of all. He loaded thofe of Epidaurus with great prefents for the deity who prefides over the city, as well as over health, but reproached them at the fame time. Æfculapius, fays he, has fhowed me but very little indulgence, in not preferving the life of a friend, who was as dear to me as myfelf. In private, he difcovered a great friendfhip for fuch of the deputies of Greece, as came congratulate him on his victories, and his happy return; and he reftored them all the ftatues, and other curiofities, which Xerxes had carried out of Greece, that were found in Sufa, Babylon, Taffagarda, and other places. We are told, that among thefe were the ftatues of Harmodrius and Ariftogiton, and that they were brought back to Athens.

The Ambaffadors from Corinth having offered him, in the name of their city, the freedom of it, he laughed at an offer which feemed altogether unworthy of one who had attained fo exalted a pitch of grandeur and power. However, when Alexander was told that Corinth had granted this privilege to Hercules only, he accepted it with joy; and piqued himfelf upon treading in his fteps, and refembling him in all things. But, cries Seneca, in what did this frantick young man, with whom fuccefsful time paffed for virtue, refemble Hecules? The latter, free from all felf-interefted views, travelled through the world, merely to ferve the feveral nations he vifited, and to purge the earth of fuch robbers as infested it ; whereas Alexander, who is justly entitled the plunderer of nation, made his glory to consist in carrying desolation into all places, and in rendering himself the terror of mankind.

At the same time he wrote a letter, which was to have been read publickly in the assembly of the Olympick games, whereby the several cities of Greece were commanded to permit all exiles to return into their native country, those excepted who had committed sacrilege, or any other crime deserving death ; and ordered Antipater to employ an armed force against such cities as should refuse to obey. This letter was read in the assembly. But as for the Athenians and Etolians, they did not think themselves obliged to put orders in execution, which seemed to interfere with their liberty.

During almost a year which Alexander continued in Babylon, he revolved a great number of projects in his mind ; such as to go round Africa by sea ; to make a complete discovery of all the nations lying round the Caspian sea, and inhabiting its coasts ; to conquer Arabia; to make war with Carthage, and to subdue the rest of Europe. The very thoughts of sitting still fatigued him, and the great vivacity of his imagination and ambition would never suffer him to be at rest ; nay, could he have conquered the whole world, he would have sought a new one, to satiate the avidity of his desires.

The embellishing of Babylon also employed his thoughts very much. Finding it surpassed in extent, in conveniency, and in whatever can be wished, either for the necessities or pleasures of life, all the other cities of the East, he resolved to make it the seat of his empire ; and for that purpose, was desirous of.

adding

adding to it all the conveniences and ornaments possible.

This city, as well as the country round about it, had suffered prodigiously by the breaking of the bank or dike of the Euphrates, at the head of the canal called Pallacopa. The river running out of its usual channel by this breach, overflowed the whole country; and forcing its way perpetually, the breach grew at last so wide, that it would have cost almost as much to repair the bank, as the raising of it had done at first. So little water was left in the channel of the Euphrates about Babylon, that there was scarce depth enough for small boats, which consequently was of great prejudice to the city.

Alexander undertook to remedy this, for which purpose he embarked upon the Euphrates, in order to take a view of the place. It was on this occasion that he reproached, in a ludicrous, insulting tone of voice, the Magi and Chaldeans who accompanied him, for the vanity of their predictions, since, notwithstanding the ill omens they had endeavoured to terrify him with (as if he had been a credulous woman) he however had entered Babylon, and was returned from it very safe. Attentive to nothing but the subject of his voyage, he went and reviewed the breach, and gave the proper orders for repairing and restoring it to its former condition.

This work, after having been carried on the length of a league and an half, was stopped by difficulties owing to the nature of the soil; and the death of this prince, which happened soon after, put an end to this project.

Another design which Alexander meditated, and had most at heart, was repairing the temple of Belus.

Xerxes

Xerxes had demolished it in his return from Greece, and it had lain in ruins ever since. Now Alexander was resolved, not only to rebuild it, but even to raise a much more magnificent temple. Accordingly, he had caused all the rubbish to be removed; and finding that the Magi, to whose care he had left this, went on but slowly, he made his soldiers work. Notwithstanding ten thousand of them were daily employed at it, for two months succeffively, the work was not finished at the death of this prince, so prodigious were its ruins. When it came to the turn of the Jewish soldiers, who were in his army, to work as the rest had done, they could not be prevailed upon to give their assistance; but excused themselves with saying, that as idolatry was forbid by the tenets of their religion, they therefore were not allowed to assist in building of a temple, designed for idolatrous worship; and accordingly not one lent a hand on this occasion. They were punished for disobedience, but all to no purpose; so that, at last, Alexander admiring their perseverance, discharged, and sent them home.

Athough Alexander employed himself in the works above mentioned, during his stay in Babylon, he spent the greatest part of his time in such pleasures as that city afforded; and was daily solemnizing new festivals, and perpetually at new banquets, in which he quaffed with his usual intemperance. After having spent a whole night in carousing, a second was proposed to him. He met accordingly, and there were twenty guests at table. He drank to the health of every person in company, and then pledged them severally. After this, calling for Hercules's cup, which held six bottles, it was filled, when he poured

down, drinking to a Macedonian of
/, Proteas by name, and afterwards
1 again, in the same furious bumper.
)oner swallowed it, but he fell upon the
ere then," cries Seneca, describing the
)f drunkenness, " is this hero; invinci-
the toils of prodigious marches, to the
f sieges and combats, to the moft violent
)f heat and cold; here he lies, conquer-
intemperance, and struck to the earth
al cup of Hercules."
dition he was seized with a violent fe-
ied half dead to his palace. The fever
hough with some good intervals, in
ve the necessary orders for the sailing of
l the marching of his land-forces, being
e should soon recover. But at last,
elf past all hopes, and his voice begin-
he drew his ring from his finger, and
rdiccas with orders to convey his corpse
e of Ammon.
anding his great weakness, he however
h death, and raising himself upon his
nted his soldiers (to whom he could not
t testimony of friendship) his dying hand
er this, his principal courtiers asking
t the empire; he answered, TO THE
RTHY; adding, that he foresaw the
iis would give occasion to strange funer-
er his disease. And Perdiccas, enquir-
what time they should pay him divine
eplied, WHEN YOU ARE HAPPY.
his last words, and soon after he expired.
ty-two years and eight months old,
X which

which he had reigned twelve. He died in the middle of the fpring, the firſt year of the cxivth Olympiad.*

No one, fufpected then that Alexander had been poifoned; and yet it is at this time that fuch reports generally prevail. But the ſtate of his body proved that he did not die that way; all his chief officers difagreeing amongſt themfelves, the corpfe, though it lay quite neglected for feveral days in Babylon, which ſtands in a hot climate, did not fhow the leaſt fymptoms of putrefaction. The true poifon which brought him to his end was wine, which has killed many thoufands befides Alexander. It was neverthelefs, believed afterwards, that this prince had been poifoned by the treachery of Antipater's fons; that Caffander, the eldeſt of them brought the poifon from Greece; that Iolas, his younger brother, threw the fatal draught into Alexander's cup, of which he was the bearer; and that he cunningly chofe the time of the great feaſt mentioned before, in order that the prodigious quantity of wine he then drank, might conceal the true caufe of his death. The ſtate of Antipater's affairs at that time, gave fome grounds for this fufpicion. He was perfuaded that he had been recalled with no other view than to ruin him, becaufe of his mal-adminiſtration during his vice-royalty; and it was not altogether improbable, that he commanded his fons to commit a crime, which would fave his own life, by taking away that of his fovereign. An undoubted circumſtance is, that he could never wafh out this ſtain; and that as long as he lived, the Macedonians deteſted him as a traitor who had poifoned their king. Ariſtotle was alfo fufpected, but with no great foundation.

The

* *A. M.* 3613. *Ant. J. C.* 326.

The moment that Alexander's death was known, the whole place echoed with cries and groans. The vanquished bewailed him with as many tears as the victors. The grief for his death occasioning the remembrance of his many good qualities, all his faults were forgotten. The Persians declared him to have been the most just, the kindest sovereign that ever reigned over them; the Macedonians the best, the most valiant prince in the universe; and all exclaimed against the gods, for having enviously bereaved mankind of him, in the flower of his age, and the height of his fortune. The Macedonians imagined they saw Alexander, with a firm and intrepid air, still lead them on to battle, besiege cities, climb walls, and reward such as had distinguished themselves. They then reproached themselves for having refused him divine honors; and confessed they had been ungrateful and impious, for bereaving him of a name he so justly merited.

After paying him this homage of veneration and tears, they turned their whole thoughts and reflections on themselves, and on the sad condition to which they were reduced by Alexander's death. They considered, that they were on the farther side (with respect to Macedonia) of the Euphrates, without a leader to head them; and surrounded with enemies, who abhorred their new yoke. As the king died without nominating his successor, a dreadful futurity presented itself to their imagination; and exhibited nothing but divisions, civil wars, and a fatal necessity of still shedding their blood, and of opening their former wounds, not to conquer Asia, but only to give a king to it; and to raise to the throne perhaps some mean officer or wicked wretch.

This

This great mourning was not confined merely to Babylon, but spread over all the province, and the news of it soon reached Darius's mother. One of her daughters was with her, who being still inconsolable for the death of Hephæstion her husband, the sight of the public calamity recalled all her private woes. But Sysigambis bewailed the several misfortunes of her family; and this new affliction awaked the remembrance of all its former sufferings. One would have thought that Darius was but just dead, and that this unfortunate mother solemnized the funeral of two sons at the same time. She wept the living no less than the dead; who now, would she say, will take care of my daughters; Where shall we find another Alexander? She would fancy she saw them again reduced to a state of captivity, and that they had lost their kingdom a second time; but with this difference, that now Alexander was gone, they had no refuge left. At last, she sunk under her grief. This princess, who had borne with patience the death of her father, her husband, of four of her brothers, who were murdered in one day by Ochus, and, to say all in one word, that of Darius her son, and the ruin of her family; though she had, submitted patiently to all these losses, she however had not strength of mind sufficient to support herself after the death of Alexander. She would not take any sustenance, and starved herself to death, to avoid her surviving this last calamity.

After Alexander's death, great contentions arose among the Macedonians, about appointing him a successor. After seven days spent in confusion and disputes, it was agreed that Arideus,

bastard

bastard brother to Alexander should be declared king; and that in case Roxana, who was eight months gone with child, should be delivered of a son he should share the throne in conjunction with Arideus, and that Perdiccas should have the care of both; for Arideus was a weak man, and wanted a guardian as much as a child.

The Egyptians and Chaldeans having embalmed the king's corpse after their manner, Arideus was appointed to convey it to the temple of Jupiter-Ammon. Two whole years were employed in preparing for this magnificent funeral, which made Olympias bewail the fate of her son, who having had the ambition to rank himself among the gods, was so long deprived of burial, a privilege allowed to the meanest of mortals.

FINIS.

JOSEPH J. TODD,

HAS FOR SALE,

At the BIBLE and ANCHOR,

in PROVIDENCE,

A well assorted Collection of BOOKS, *consisting of the most approved Authors in*

HISTORY,	SURGERY,
VOYAGES,	CHEMISTRY,
TRAVELS,	GEOGRAPHY,
LIVES,	HUSBANDRY,
MEMOIRS,	NAVIGATION,
ANTIQUITIES,	ARTS,
PHILOSOPHY,	SCIENCES,
NOVELS,	ARCHITECTURE,
DIVINITY,	MISCELLANIES,
LAW,	POETRY,
PHYSIC,	PLAYS, &c. &c.

Which are selling on as good Terms as at any Bookstore whatever.

Social and private Libraries, and Country Merchants supplied on generous Terms.

Circulating Library,

For Town and Country, consisting of near two Thousand Volumes of the latest European and American Publications; to which Additions are continually making.

*** CASH, or new Books, given in Exchange for old Books. *June* 3, 1796.

www.ingramcontent.com/pod-product-compliance
Lightning Source LLC
Chambersburg PA
CBHW021354230426
43666CB00006B/518